TRUE TALES OF THE WILD WEST

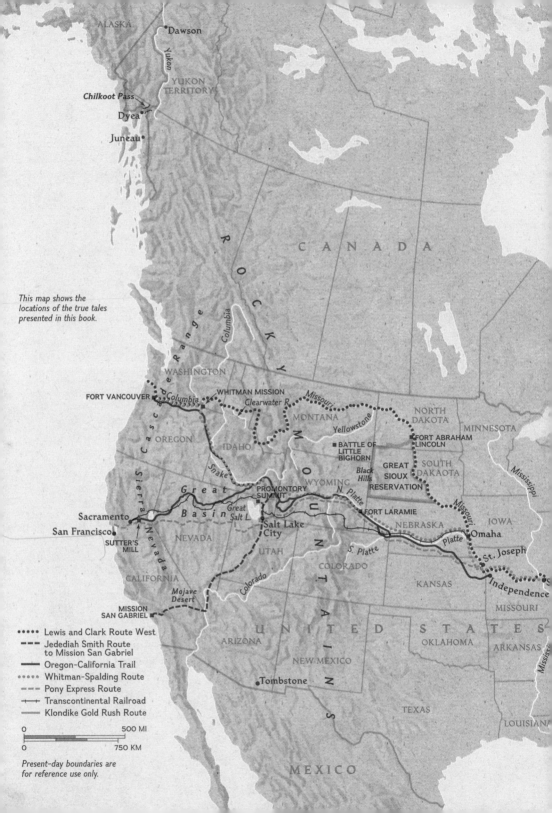

This map shows the locations of the true tales presented in this book.

**ALASKA**

Dawson

**YUKON TERRITORY**

*Chilkoot Pass*
Dyea
Juneau

**CANADA**

**ROCKY**

Columbia

**WASHINGTON**

FORT VANCOUVER
Columbia
WHITMAN MISSION
*Clearwater R.*
*Missouri*

**NORTH DAKOTA**

FORT ABRAHAM LINCOLN

**MINNESOTA**

**OREGON**

**IDAHO**

*Snake*

**MONTANA**

*Yellowstone*

BATTLE OF LITTLE BIGHORN

*Black Hills*

GREAT SIOUX RESERVATION

**SOUTH DAKOTA**

*Missouri*

**MOUNTAINS**

Great Basin

PROMONTORY SUMMIT

*Great Salt L.*

Salt Lake City

**WYOMING**

*N. Platte*

FORT LARAMIE

**NEBRASKA**

*Platte*

Omaha

**IOWA**

*Missouri*

St. Joseph

*Mississippi*

Sacramento
San Francisco
SUTTER'S MILL

**NEVADA**

**UTAH**

*Colorado*

*S. Platte*

**COLORADO**

**KANSAS**

Independence

**MISSOURI**

**CALIFORNIA**

*Mojave Desert*

MISSION SAN GABRIEL

**ARIZONA**

**UNITED STATES**

**NEW MEXICO**

Tombstone

**OKLAHOMA**

**ARKANSAS**

*Mississippi*

**TEXAS**

**LOUISIANA**

**MEXICO**

Sierra Nevada

Cascade Range

•••• Lewis and Clark Route West
--- Jedediah Smith Route to Mission San Gabriel
— Oregon-California Trail
•••• Whitman-Spalding Route
--- Pony Express Route
+-+ Transcontinental Railroad
— Klondike Gold Rush Route

0        500 MI
0        750 KM

*Present-day boundaries are for reference use only.*

# TRUE TALES
## OF THE
# WILD WEST

## PAUL ROBERT WALKER

NATIONAL GEOGRAPHIC

WASHINGTON, D.C.

TO MY CHILDREN, DEVIN AND DARIEL,
WHO LOVE TO EXPLORE THE WEST.

Wagons head west across the Oregon Trail in this painting
by William Henry Jackson.

I WOULD LIKE TO THANK THE FOLLOWING INDIVIDUALS WHO READ STORIES IN THEIR FIELDS OF
EXPERTISE AND OFFERED HELPFUL SUGGESTIONS: ALAN BEILHARZ, MARSHALL GOLD DISCOVERY
STATE HISTORIC PARK; HAWORTH CLOVER, JEDEDIAH SMITH SOCIETY; HOLLIS COOK, TOMBSTONE
COURTHOUSE STATE HISTORIC PARK; JOHN DOERNER, LITTLE BIGHORN BATTLEFIELD NATIONAL
MONUMENT; MICHAEL GATES, YUKON FIELD UNIT, PARKS CANADA; EUGENE HUNN, UNIVERSITY OF
WASHINGTON; JACQUELINE LEWIN, ST. JOSEPH MUSEUM; SANDRA LOWRY, FORT LARAMIE NATIONAL
HISTORIC SITE; ROGER TRICK, WHITMAN MISSION NATIONAL HISTORIC SITE; RICK WILSON, GOLDEN
SPIKE NATIONAL HISTORIC SITE.

# CONTENTS

# INTRODUCTION

THE WILD WEST IS A PLACE AND A TIME AND AN ATTITUDE. These aspects can be defined in different ways, but for this book the place is the land beyond the Mississippi River. The time is the 19th century. And the attitude is adventure, independence, and strength of character under new and difficult conditions.

The "wildness" of the West changed dramatically over the ten decades of the 19th century, as you will discover in these ten stories. When the Lewis and Clark expedition set out from their winter camp on the Missouri River in 1805, they entered an Indian world where "the foot of civillized man had never trodden," in Lewis's dramatic words. There was nothing wild in the behavior of the men in the expedition, and the Indians they met treated them in a remarkably civilized manner despite Lewis's statement. The wildness in this early period of exploration lay in the land itself, the unspoiled wilderness of western North America.

As fur trappers, missionaries, settlers, and prospectors followed in the wake of the explorers, new kinds of wildness characterized the western experience. Wild, boisterous, and sometimes violent behavior exploded in boomtowns, mining camps, and railroad tent towns. Wild warfare stained the earth with blood as the Indians fought to defend their sacred land from the white intruders. Wild enthusiasm, bravery, and hard work ultimately tamed the wilderness and connected the continent.

By 1893, white Americans had spread so completely throughout the West that historian Frederick Jackson Turner proclaimed the death of the frontier. Obviously, he did not consider the Last Frontier of the Far North, where the Klondike gold discovery of 1896 set off the last great North American gold rush—the last gasp of the Wild West spirit that brings this book to a close.

The Wild West has been called the great American myth, and the mythmaking began almost immediately at the time of the events, to be passed down in popular books, magazines, television shows, and movies. The myths are important, for they tell us much about who we think we are as a nation. But the truth is more important and more interesting, for it tells us about who we really are.

I have tried to tell these stories as truthfully as I can. I have visited the sites and consulted with experts. I have read journals, diaries, letters, newspaper accounts, and legal testimonies. As much as possible, I have allowed these remarkable men and women to tell their stories in their own words, preserving their often-eccentric spelling and punctuation to give the flavor of the time. Even so, I cannot claim that these stories are absolutely "true," because absolute truth is lost the moment an event occurs. And historical truth is always changing as we discover new evidence or look at old evidence with a new point of view.

Think for a moment about what you did yesterday. Can you remember everything you did and tell it as a story to someone else? Can you be sure everything you say is true? Now think about what you did the day before and the day before that. The truth gets harder to capture with every passing day—like chasing your own shadow under a hazy sun. That's what it is like to write history. The truth seems to dance just a step ahead, teasing us, playing with us, daring us to grab it and get it right.

I've tried to get it right in stories that bring these extraordinary places, times, and personalities alive. But there is always more truth to discover. I invite you to ask your own questions, chase your own shadows, and explore the Wild West.

*Paul Robert Walker*

Two members of the Lewis and Clark expedition battle
the churning rapids of the Columbia River.

## TALE Nº 1

# BIG RIVER

### LEWIS AND CLARK DESCEND THE COLUMBIA

**1805**

TALL, RED-HAIRED WILLIAM CLARK stood on the massive black rock with his best river pilot, Pierre Cruzatte, and gazed down into the whirling whitecapped waters below. A crowd of Indians gathered around them, wondering if these strange white-skinned visitors were really crazy enough to paddle their canoes through this evil place—where the entire force of the Columbia, largest and most powerful river in the West, squeezed between the rock and another rock just 45 yards away. The Indians didn't measure in yards, and they called the river by another name, Nch'i Wana, Big River. They were expert canoeists who knew the river as they knew themselves, and even they would not challenge the foaming waters.

Examining the volcanic cliffs above the river, Clark saw that there was no practical way to carry their heavy canoes along the shore. Fortunately the expedition reached the whirlpool in October, when the water was near its low point. It was still a frightening sight, but the only real danger, Clark thought, "was the whorls and Swills [swells] arriseing from the Compression of the water." He believed they could make it through "by good Stearing," and Pierre Cruzatte agreed. Pierre had only one good eye,

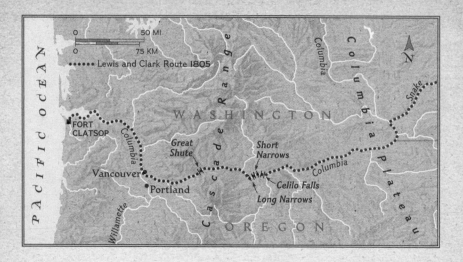

but when it came to judging a river, he could see more with one eye than most men could see with two. "I deturmined to pass through this place," Clark wrote in his journal, "notwithstanding the horrid appearance of this agitated gut Swelling, boiling & whorling in every direction."

Meriwether Lewis, the co-commander of the expedition, is not mentioned at all in Clark's description of this tense moment. Earlier that morning, Lewis had set out with three other men to get a good view of Celilo Falls, the great rapids that began this dangerous stretch of the Columbia. The expedition had been camping at the falls for two days, carefully carrying their canoes around them with help from the Indian people who lived there. Clark's diary doesn't mention Lewis again until late that afternoon, when they met at an Indian village beyond the whirlpool; so Lewis and his companions may have walked that day, scrambling up the rocky cliffs, while Clark led the rest of the expedition through the treacherous waters. But we can't know for sure, because Meriwether Lewis wrote nothing at all about his journey down the Columbia.

There is something strange about Lewis's long silence in his diary on the great river. Perhaps he was still weak from gorging on roots and salmon among the Indians west of the Continental Divide. Many of the men had gotten sick from the change of diet, so sick that whenever possible they bought dogs from the Indians and ate them instead. Then again, maybe Captain Lewis had a different kind of sickness, a sickness of the mind and spirit. Although he was a brilliant, brave man, Lewis often battled depression, and the Columbia River—powerful, mysterious, and densely populated by Indians—would have a strange effect on many whites.

Meriwether Lewis

As William Clark led the way down the Columbia on that day, October 24, 1805, he controlled the fate of the expedition's five canoes, all their supplies, and precious human lives. Although we don't know precisely who was in the canoes as they faced the whirlpool, there were 33 members of the official expedition that had left their winter camp on the Missouri River six months earlier: Lewis and Clark, three sergeants, 23 privates, and five civilians, including Clark's black slave, York, and two French-Canadian interpreters. One interpreter, Toussaint Charbonneau, had a young Shoshone wife named Sacagawea, or "Bird Woman," who carried their eight-month-old baby boy.

William Clark

Captain Lewis's big Newfoundland dog, Seaman, accompanied the expedition, too, but the journals are silent on what Seaman thought about all the dogs that were eaten along the way.

There were also two chiefs of the Nez Perce tribe, Twisted Hair and Tetoharsky, whom they had met in what is now Idaho. The chiefs had accompanied the explorers down the Clearwater and Snake Rivers into the Columbia, telling people along the way that the white men came in peace. Now they were eager to return to their homeland, for beyond the whirlpool lived an enemy tribe whose language they did not understand.

The white captains insisted that they would try to make a peace if the chiefs would stay just two nights longer. The chiefs agreed, but if they were in the canoes that October day, they must have had second thoughts as they faced the rushing waters.

Clark and Cruzatte climbed down from the big black rock and joined the rest of the expedition waiting on the shore. The day before, Lewis had

Colville Indians fish for salmon at Kettle Falls on the upper Columbia River in the painting by Paul Kane, who traveled the Columbia in 1846–47.

traded their smallest canoe, a hatchet, and a few trinkets for a new canoe made by the Indians who lived on the lower river—the same people whose territory they were now approaching. Wide in the middle and tapering at the ends, with mysterious figures carved into the bow, the canoe was "neeter made than any I have ever Seen and Calculated to ride the waves," Clark observed. It would have to ride them now, and so would the other canoes they had made themselves—rough, heavy, and not so neat at all.

As the Indians watched in wonder from the top of the big black rock, certain the white men would be sucked into the river and seen no more, the explorers paddled their canoes into the boiling, whirling waters. Tossed like toys on the angry waves, soaked by the cold Columbia, they strained against their paddles, steering the course that Clark and Cruzatte had chosen, desperately pulling their big canoes out of the whirlpool toward calmer water beyond. With a combination of luck, skill, and bravery, all five canoes made it through safely, though even a tough frontiersman like William Clark had to admit that the whirling waters were much worse than they had appeared from the top of the rock.

This was only the beginning. Beyond the whirlpool—which Clark called the Short Narrows—the river widened to some 200 yards for a two-mile stretch that led to "a verry bad place" where two islands of rocks divided the current and created treacherous rapids. The same low-water conditions that allowed the explorers to pass through the whirlpool made rocky places like this even more dangerous. Clark ordered those who could not swim to walk along the shore, carrying the party's guns, ammunition, and papers, while the men who could swim guided the canoes two at a time through the rapids.

Their hard work was rewarded when they reached an Indian village of wooden houses, the first wooden houses they had seen since leaving Illinois almost 18 months earlier. This was the outpost of a new culture, the Chinookan-speaking people of the lower Columbia.

The explorers had heard rumors that Indians of the lower river intended to kill them, but they were received kindly in the village of wooden houses. Chinook people had been trading with white men for more than a decade, ever since the first American and British ships had entered the mouth of the Columbia in 1792. The explorers saw clear signs of white influence: a new copper tea kettle, copper beads, and a light-skinned child who looked to be born of a white father and an Indian mother. "The fairness of its Skin, & rosey colour," wrote Private Joseph

Whitehouse, one of several other men who kept a journal, "convinced us that . . . white Men trade among them."

A great chief from the lower river came to visit the explorers at their camp near the village, and the two white captains forged a peace between him and the Nez Perce chiefs. It was a night for celebration. Pierre Cruzatte played the violin, and the visitors danced for their hosts. Although Clark doesn't mention him on this particular night, his muscular black slave, York, was a wonderful dancer, and the big man entranced Indian people throughout the journey, not only for his black skin and tightly curled hair but also for his grace and agility.

The captains rose early the next morning to examine the challenge ahead: another set of treacherous rapids that Clark called the Long Narrows. Here again the nonswimmers carried valuable goods by land while the swimmers ran the canoes through the wild and turbulent water. One canoe almost sank, and all its contents were soaked; other canoes were damaged running over the rocks. Even so, Clark felt "extreamly gratified and pleased" once they were safely below the rapids. That afternoon, the explorers said good-bye to the friendly Nez Perce chiefs, who had traded for horses so they could return to their people.

The expedition camped for three nights to repair the canoes and hunt in the foothills of the mountains. When they continued down the river, they saw more white-manufactured goods among the Indians: a sailor hat and jacket, a British musket, a sword, and brass tea kettles. At a "friendly Village," the chief opened his medicine bag and proudly showed the visitors 14 fingers he had cut off from enemies he had killed in battle.

Now the mountain walls rose higher around them, pine and oak trees dotting the cliffs. They were entering the heart of the breathtaking Columbia Gorge, where the mighty river cut its way through the mountains on its relentless journey to the sea. With each mile, the land grew wetter and greener, and the trees grew taller as pine and oak gave way to towering spruce and fir. Finally, on the evening of October 30, the expedition reached the last wild rapids of the Columbia. They called it the Great Shute, but the rapids and the mountains both became known as the Cascades. Here "the water of this great river Compressed within the Space of 150 paces," Clark wrote, "in which there is great numbers of both large and Small rocks, water passing with great velocity forming [foaming] & boiling in a most horrible manner, with a fall of about 20 feet."

According to Private Whitehouse, the Indians who lived just above the falls "made signs to us as we passed along. . . that they thought & supposed that we had rained down from the Clouds." These Indians knew that white people existed, but what amazed them was that these white men came down the river from the east, rather than approaching from the ocean on the west, and they did it at a time of low water when the rocks were exposed and the rapids deadly.

As they descended these last rapids, William Clark carefully observed the Indian people who came to visit and trade with them. Like some of the Indians he had met farther up the river, the lower Columbia people deformed the heads of women by pressing their skulls between two boards during infancy to create a long, straight profile, which they considered a mark of beauty.

A page from William Clark's journal depicting head-flattening among the Chinook Indians.

For three days, the explorers worked their way through the Great Shute. Finally, on the morning of Sunday, November 3, 1805, they awoke on the fog-shrouded shore of the lower Columbia, where the broad river rose and fell with the tide of the Pacific Ocean, churning in the cold gray mists some 100 miles away. Other adventures awaited before they would see the crashing ocean waves, but on that foggy morning, the explorers knew they would reach their goal. They had run safely through the wild rapids of the Big River, the first whites to travel this dangerous yet beautiful path, the first whites to travel from the Mississippi Valley to the Far West. They would not be the last.

## Historical Note

The journey of Lewis and Clark was the first American expedition to explore the lands between the Mississippi River and the Pacific Ocean. A large part of these lands, stretching from the Mississippi to the Rocky Mountains, had become U.S. territory through the Louisiana Purchase in 1803, just a year before the expedition began. West of the Rockies, the land that now makes up the states of Idaho, Oregon, and Washington and part of western Canada were claimed by the United States, Britain, Russia, and Spain. The first ship to enter the treacherous mouth of the Columbia River was an American ship from Boston. In 1792, it sailed a few miles up the river and traded for furs with the Indians before continuing on across the Pacific to China. The American captain, Robert Gray, named the river after his ship, the *Columbia Rediviva,* meaning "Columbia Reborn."

A few months later, a small British ship sailed about a hundred miles up the river just past the present sites of Vancouver, Washington, and Portland, Oregon. The British also claimed the river and the land around it, and drew a fairly accurate chart of the lower river. On the last day of our story, November 3, 1805, the Lewis and Clark expedition paddled down the river to this same area. At that moment, the explorers knew that it was possible to travel from the eastern United States all the way to the Pacific. They also knew that there was no easy route.

Before Lewis and Clark, Americans and Europeans believed there might be an all-water route called the Northwest Passage. Lewis and Clark followed the Missouri River—believed to be the beginning of the Northwest Passage—as far as they could go. They discovered that the western journey required them to make a long and difficult overland trek across the Rocky Mountains before reaching the rivers that ran westward into the Columbia and on to the Pacific. They spent a cold, wet winter in a wooden stockade called Fort Clatsop before heading back east in March 1806.

The Lewis and Clark expedition opened the West for American traders and settlers. The men of the expedition treated the Indians with respect and courtesy, and in most cases the Indians treated them with great generosity in return. Without the help of the Indian people, it seems unlikely that the expedition would have succeeded. Unfortunately, these good relationships would not last. In time, the careful, well-disciplined expedition would be followed by tens of thousands of whites looking for a better life in the West. The first great destination for American settlers was the Willamette Valley of Oregon, just south of present-day Portland. Although the famous Oregon Trail followed a different route across the mountains than the route of Lewis and Clark, all of the settlers had to travel down the Columbia and—until a toll road was built in 1846—they had to shoot the wild and dangerous rapids of the Big River.

*This story is based primarily on William Clark's journal. Meriwether Lewis did not write in his journal during the trip down the Columbia— at least no such writing has ever been found. Three journals written by other members of the expedition describe the same events in less detail and occasionally offer an interesting piece of additional information— such as Joseph Whitehouse's description of the white-skinned child and the description by both Whitehouse and Sergeant John Ordway of the Indians who thought the expedition had "rained down from the Clouds."*

Jedediah Smith and his party of trappers cross the blistering desert
on the trip that ultimately took them to the Spanish missions of California.

## TALE Nº 2

# NO WATER

### JEDEDIAH SMITH CROSSES THE DESERT

1826

JEDEDIAH SMITH SQUINTED at the damp sand where the little stream disappeared. He had been following this stream and others like it for three days now, ever since crossing a range of mountains into a low, dry country. The other streams disappeared in the sand as well. They were the strangest mountain streams he had ever seen, and Smith had seen a lot of mountain streams.

Jedediah and his band of fur trappers were looking for beavers, whose soft fur was worn by fashionable people in Europe as hats, coats, muffs, and collars. Smith's party was a long way from Europe and they were definitely not fashionable, but beavers were their business and beavers didn't live in sand. "As it was useless for me to look for Beaver where there was no water," Smith later wrote, "I retraced my steps to where there was water and grass."

In modern terms, we might say that Smith and his party were lost, except you can't really be lost when you don't know where you are trying to go. They were exploring unknown country, and they had heard rumors of a great river that ran through this country from the Rocky Mountains all the way to the Pacific Ocean. It was called the Buenaventura, Spanish

This 1826 map shows the mythical Buenaventura River.

for "Good Fortune," and it was shown on all the maps. Unfortunately for Jedediah Smith and his trappers, the river did not exist—except in the imagination of the mapmakers.

The next morning, the trappers headed toward the southwest because the land looked lowest in that direction, and low land usually contained water and perhaps a river. They traveled 20 miles through searing heat, leading their horses packed with dried buffalo meat and other supplies. They had been on the trail for a month now, and the meat was almost gone. The horses were exhausted, and several would collapse by the end of the day. The men were exhausted, too.

There were about 18 trappers with Jedediah that year, two of them traveling with Indian wives and sons. There were also two other Indian women whom the trappers had rescued from the Ute tribe earlier in their journey. All of them depended on Jedediah Smith to find the way. But when Smith held his small telescope to his eye and gazed into the distance, he found "to my great Surprise instead of a River an immense sand plain . . . where the utmost view with my Glass could not embrace any appearance of water."

Although he didn't know it, Smith had led his party into the Great Basin in what is now western Utah. In this region, no water ever reaches the sea. Instead, the trickling streams disappear into sandy wastes or salty lakes, where the water evaporates in the hot desert sun. The Great Basin is a place where rivers go to die, and in the years to come many white travelers would die there as well. But Jedediah Smith was no ordinary traveler.

Heading south, Smith climbed a high hill and caught sight of distant trees through his telescope. Trees meant water, so he led his men in that direction the following day. They found a creek that showed signs of beavers, and they began to see signs of Indians, too, though most of them had fled at the approach of the white men. Two curious Indians remained behind, but they began to run at full speed as soon as the whites caught sight of them. Two trappers jumped on their horses and rode after them. "The probability is they had never seen or heard of horses before," Smith reasoned, "and of course were much frightened when they saw the men as it seemed to them sailing through the air." By the time the trappers caught them, the Indians were so afraid that Smith just gave them a few small presents and let them go.

The men trapped on the creek for three days, but they found no beavers. So they followed the creek back into the mountains and crossed another range to yet another stream. Here the two men with Indian wives demanded to return the way they had come, but Smith refused. He had set out to explore new lands and find valuable furs, and he wasn't about to turn back now. These men were "free trappers" who could come and go as they pleased, so they took their families and headed back toward the east. That night, a third man stole a horse, a rifle, and ammunition and ran off with the two Indian women rescued from the Utes. Now there was just Jedediah Smith and about 15 other men, pushing on into the unknown.

The buffalo meat was gone, and the trappers faced starvation in a land with few natural resources. Just when the situation looked desperate, they came upon a wide stream running toward the southwest. Smith named it the Adams River after President John Quincy Adams, but it is known as the Virgin River today. Following the river, they found dried cornstalks that had been planted by Indians several years before. The men "could hardly believe it possible that corn had ever been planted in this lonely country."

On their second day following the river, they met the Indians themselves. These were Paiutes, the same tribe they had met earlier, but these people were braver than the others. As a sign of friendship, one Paiute man held out a rabbit he had killed. When Smith took the rabbit and touched the man gently as a gesture of thanks, the whites were surrounded by friendly Indians. In return for a few trinkets, including pieces of metal that they could use for arrowheads, the Paiutes gave the trappers corn and pumpkins that they had "close at hand," hidden perhaps in a cool spot away from the desert sun.

Smith later wrote that the simple food might seem "indifferent . . . to him who has never made his pillow of the sand of the plain or him who would

Jedediah Smith

consider it a hardship to go without his dinner yet to us weary and hungry in the desert it was a feast a treat that made my party in their sudden hilarity and Glee present a lively contrast to the moody desponding silence of the night before." The trappers stayed for three days among the Paiutes, resting and trading for corn to carry with them on their journey.

Still following the Virgin River, the trappers reached another Paiute village, where they met two men from the neighboring Mohave tribe. Through signs, the Mohaves told Smith that there was a bigger river one day's journey to the south, and farther down the big river there was plenty of beaver. Trapping beaver all winter in this warm climate sounded good to Jedediah, so he followed the Mohaves to the big river, which he correctly guessed was the "Colorado of the west."

Led by the Indian guides, Smith's party crossed the Colorado on a raft made of driftwood and finally reached a large Mohave settlement scattered along the river in what is now northern Arizona. The Indians treated them "with great kindness," offering melons and roasted pumpkins to the hungry visitors. The Mohave were taller and lighter-skinned than most Indian people. They had contact with Spanish explorers and knew of the Spanish missions in California, so they were not as amazed by the whites as the Paiutes were. The Mohave even had horses, and Smith traded some of his tired animals for fresh ones.

Despite the promises of the Indians, Smith found no signs of beaver along the Colorado. It was mid-October now. If they tried to return the way they had come, there would be too much snow by the time they reached the Rocky Mountains. So Smith decided to push on and cross the desert to the Spanish settlements in California, where he hoped to resupply himself for a journey to the north. "I expected to find beaver," he wrote, "and in all probability some considerable river heading up in the vicinity of the Great Salt Lake." After two months on the desert trail, Jedediah Smith was still chasing the mythical Buenaventura.

Smith and his men made another raft to cross the Colorado and headed alone into the desert—or at least they thought they were alone. That first night, Smith's most valuable horse was stolen. The next day he was unable to follow the directions he had received from the Mohave, and there was no water to be found. Smith wondered if the Mohave people who had seemed so friendly had actually sent him "into the desert to perish." Despite his suspicions, he had no choice but to return to the precious water of the Colorado. There he rested for awhile at an even larger Mohave village, where he recovered his stolen horse. It was the time of the melon harvest, and the Mohaves generously piled hundreds of melons outside Smith's tent.

Mission San Gabriel, painted in 1832 by Ferdinand Deppe

At this village, Smith met two Indians who had run away from the California missions. Runaways were a constant problem at the Spanish missions, for many Indians tired of forced labor and fled to live among free tribes like the Mohave. Either Smith was very persuasive or these particular runaways were homesick, because he managed to persuade them to act as his guides. Crossing the "dry rocky sandy Barren desert" the Indians and trappers picked up the trail of another strange river, which Smith named the Inconstant for its habit of disappearing into the sand. Fortunately, it also came back out of the sand, and Smith, with his Indian guides, was able to follow this river—which we call the Mojave—to what is now Victorville, California.

Finally, in late November, the party descended from the high desert into the fertile San Bernardino Valley, where they saw clear trails of horses and "fine herds of Cattle in many directions." They had reached the outskirts of the Spanish mission world, and Jedediah Smith's diary reveals that he was more afraid of what he might find in that world than what he had faced in the wilderness. "As those sure evidences of Civilization passed in sight they awakened many emotions in my mind and some of them not the most pleasant. . . . They reminded me that I was approaching a country inhabited by Spaniards . . . a people of different religion from mine. They might perhaps consider me a spy imprison me persecute me for the sake of religion or detain me in prison to the ruin of my business."

The Spanish had always been hostile toward American visitors, and though Mexico had won its independence from Spain five years earlier, Smith was right to be concerned. He would have a difficult time explaining what he was doing in California, but he could worry about that later. First his hungry men had to eat. Using "all the precaution necessary in approaching Buffalo," Smith killed one of the cattle, but he kept the branded skin so he could repay the owner if he ever met him.

Two days later, they reached a mission outpost, where the Indians stared at them in amazement. No white man had ever come into the mission from the desert. They believed only Indians lived in that direction, so they wondered "how indians could be so white." Smith was no less amazed by the beautiful green landscape that "seemed to us enchantment" after the "interminable waste of sands."

Later that same day, Smith reached San Gabriel, then among the largest and most prosperous of the California missions. The kindly Spanish priest was as amazed as the Indians to see the tall American in a leather hunting shirt who had appeared as if by magic from the east. Jedediah Smith and his men were the first Americans to reach California by land. Although neither the priest, nor the Indians, nor even Smith himself understood it on that November day in 1826, they were the beginning of a great migration that would take the American people across the continent, settling the land from sea to shining sea.

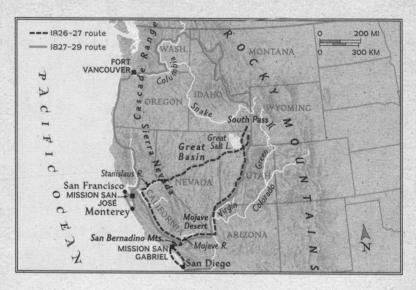

**Historical Note**

Called the "Greatest American Traveler," Jedediah Smith was born in New York State in 1799. He joined a fur-trading expedition led by William H. Ashley in 1822, traveling from St. Louis up the Missouri River, much the same path that Lewis and Clark had taken at the beginning of their journey. During the next decade, Smith saw more of the West than any other white man, probably even more than any Indian.

In 1824, following advice from Indians, Smith and a band of trappers found a gentle sloping pass across the Rockies in what is now Wyoming. Known as South Pass, this route had been used from west to east during the winter of 1812–13 by a group of fur traders returning from an unsuccessful colony at Astoria, Oregon. The location of the pass had been lost, and it was Smith's rediscovery that paved the way for tens of thousands of people who later headed West in covered wagons over the Oregon-California Trail.

In the summer of 1826, Ashley sold his fur company to Smith and two other men at an annual meeting, or rendezvous, of trappers in what is now southern Idaho. While Smith's two partners headed north into well-watered country where they could expect rich trapping, Smith headed toward the southwest "to be the first to view a country on which the eyes of a white man had never gazed and to follow the course of rivers that run through a new land." In fact, two Spanish priests had led an expedition through part of this country in 1776, but Smith had no way of knowing that. It was these priests who gave the name Río Buenaventura to what we now call the Green River. In the years that followed, poor mapmaking and wishful thinking created a mythical river that ran directly from the Rockies to the Pacific Ocean.

After reaching California— and explaining his way out of trouble with the Mexican authorities— Smith and his trappers traveled north up the Central Valley where they finally found some beaver. Leaving most of his men on the Stanislaus River, Smith and two others became the first whites to cross the Sierra Nevada and the blistering Nevada desert as they headed for the annual fur-

trading rendezvous. There, Smith recruited a group of trappers, obtained enough supplies to last for two years, and immediately headed back to California. This time the Mohave Indians—who had had a bad experience with other trappers since Smith left— attacked his party, killing ten men and two Indian women who accompanied them.

Smith continued to California with the survivors, met his men on the Stanislaus River, and once again talked his way out of trouble with the authorities. He traded furs for horses and drove the herd all the way up the coast to Oregon, where his party was again attacked by Indians, who killed 15 of his men. Smith escaped both attacks, but his luck ran out in 1831 when he was killed by Comanches while leading a caravan on the Santa Fe Trail. It would be another decade before white Americans would explore the Great Basin and follow his overland journey to California.

*This story is based on Smith's journal of the 1826 journey, which was discovered in 1967 in a simple cardboard box in the attic of a house in St. Louis.*

"Narcissa Whitman Meets the Horribles," by John F. Clymer,
captures the wild greeting orchestrated by trappers and Indians for
the first white women to cross the Rocky Mountains.

IN 1831, FOUR NEZ PERCE INDIANS ACCOMPANIED A FUR CARAVAN TO ST. LOUIS TO FIND OUT MORE ABOUT THE WAY WHITE PEOPLE LIVED AND WORSHIPED GOD. MISSIONARIES HEADED WEST TO BRING THE "WHITE MAN'S BOOK OF HEAVEN."

## TALE № 3

# INDEPENDENCE DAY

## NARCISSA AND ELIZA CROSS THE ROCKIES

1836

THE AMERICAN FUR COMPANY CARAVAN headed west under the arching blue sky of what is now Wyoming. To the north were the towering snowcapped peaks of the Wind River Range, to the south the rugged, eroded Oregon Bluffs. And to the east—behind them now— was a gentle, sloping saddle of land called South Pass, an opening in the mountain divide between rivers that ran into the Atlantic Ocean and rivers that ran into the Pacific.

It was July 4, 1836, the 60th birthday of the United States of America. What made this day so special, however, was a different kind of independence and freedom: Traveling with the caravan was a small party of missionaries, including Narcissa Whitman and Eliza Spalding, the first white women to cross the Rocky Mountains.

Earlier in the journey, the missionaries had two wagons, a large one for supplies and a smaller one that allowed the women some rest from the grueling hours on horseback. They had left the big wagon behind for the mountain crossing, and the small wagon was now so packed with supplies that there was no room for passengers. So the ladies rode sidesaddle in their long, billowing dresses, the way a proper white woman was supposed to ride.

For Eliza, the jarring journey must have been painful. She was frail to begin with, and she had been feeling sick for some time now from eating a steady diet of nothing but buffalo meat. Narcissa liked buffalo meat, and she thought the journey was making her stronger every day. Just the week before, she had written, "My health is excellent, so long as I have buffalo meat I do not wish anything else."

Narcissa Whitman

Suddenly, beneath the late afternoon sun, some 15 riders on horseback appeared on the trail, whooping wildly and shooting their rifles. "As they came in sight over the hills," remembered William Gray, a single man who accompanied the two missionary couples, "they all gave a yell, such as hunters and Indians only can give; whiz, whiz came their balls over our heads, and on they came."

A frightened cry rose among the travelers, and they scrambled to defend themselves. But as the riders drew closer, the captain of the fur caravan noticed a white flag on the end of a gun. These were not hostile warriors, but a mixed group of white trappers and friendly Nez Perce Indians who had come to welcome them, Western-style.

Marcus Whitman

"It was difficult to tell which was most crazy," wrote Gray, "the horse or the rider; such hopping, hooting, running, jumping, yelling, jumping sage brush, whirling around. . . ." The riders were so wild they had no time to reload their guns, but the fur traders returned the greeting, shooting rifle balls over the heads of the welcoming party. Neither Narcissa nor Eliza had ever seen anything like this in the East!

The arrival of the caravan was always big news for the trappers and Indians waiting at the annual rendezvous, where they traded their furs for manufactured goods and whiskey brought by the caravan. The traders had sent a messenger ahead to announce their coming, and the fact that two white women were with the caravan this year was such big news that these men decided to greet them. Many trappers hadn't seen a white woman in years, and few Indians had ever seen a white woman.

Two days later, the whole caravan—missionaries, fur company, and welcoming party—arrived at the great rendezvous on the Green River, spread over a vast prairie in the shadow of the Wind River Range. There were about 100 American trappers that year, some 50 French Canadians, and 500 or 600 Indians from various tribes, mostly Nez Perce, Bannock, Salish, and Shoshone. The Nez Perce and Shoshone had helped the Lewis and Clark expedition three decades earlier, and all these tribes had come to know the white trappers well. But the idea of white women was so amazing that the Indians could hardly believe their eyes, creating a scene that Narcissa described in a letter written from the rendezvous:

> As soon as I alighted from my horse, I was met by a company of native women, one after the other, shaking hands and salluting me with a most hearty kiss. This was unexpected and affected me very much. They gave Sister Spaulding the same salutation. After we had been seated awhile in the midst of the gazing throng, one of the Chiefs who we had seen before came with his wife and very politely introduced her to us. They say they all like us and that we have come to live with them.

Marcus Whitman had visited the rendezvous the previous year and had taken two Nez Perce boys home with him. Narcissa watched the reunion of these boys with their own people after a year of living in the white man's world. "It was truly pleasing to see the meeting of Richard and John with their friends. Richard was affected to tears, his father is not here but several of his Band and brothers. When they met each took off his hat and shook hands as respectful as in civilized life."

This was Narcissa's first real opportunity to meet the people she had come to convert to Christianity, traveling thousands of miles on what she

Indians parade at the rendezvous of 1837 in "Cavalcade," by Alfred Jacob Miller.

called "an unheard of journey for females." But though she was impressed by the warmth and kindness of the Indians, she preferred to spend her time with the white trappers. Narcissa was an attractive and outgoing person, who liked to talk and laugh and visit. Now in the Rocky Mountain wilderness she found a parade of men vying for her attention.

William Gray thought it was "absolutely ridiculous" the way the "rough mountain hunter would touch his hat" to Narcissa as if he were a gentleman from the East. But Narcissa loved every minute of it, and she believed she was doing the work of the Lord. Many trappers attended the missionaries' religious services and asked for Bibles, although it's hard to say whether they really wanted religion or just wanted to make a good impression on Narcissa. "If we had packed one or two animals with bibles & testaments," she wrote, "we should have had abundant opportunity of disposing of them to the traders & trappers of the mountain who would have received them gratefully....We have given away all we have to spare."

Eliza Spalding was different. Although she was still feeling sick and spent long hours resting in her tent, she shared whatever time she could with the Indian women, trying to learn the Nez Perce language. This was the key to their mission, and Eliza understood it well: You can't teach people about your God unless you have words to teach them. All the missionaries would learn Nez Perce in time, but Eliza learned it first.

About six days after the missionaries arrived, the Indians staged a great procession for the visitors. The tribes were "all dressed and painted in their gayest uniforms," according to Gray, "each having a company of warriors in war garb, that is, naked, except a single cloth, and painted, carrying their war weapons, bearing their war emblems and Indian implements of music, such as skins drawn over hoops with rattles and trinkets to make a noise." When the parade was over, the Indians thronged around the missionary camp, eager to catch a glimpse of Narcissa and Eliza. "They were greatly interested with our females, cattle, and waggon," Marcus wrote. They called the wagon a "land canoe," and it was almost as strange a sight as the white women.

The missionary men used the rendezvous to gather information about possible trails to Oregon. Although Marcus had organized the expedition, Eliza's husband, Henry, was the only ordained minister among the group, and he and Marcus often argued over leadership decisions. We don't know if they argued at the rendezvous, but we do know they had completely different opinions of their pioneering journey.

"I see no reason to regret our choice of a journey by land," Whitman wrote to the missionary board that sponsored them. "In my own case & Mrs. Whitmans we are more than compensated for the journey by the improvement of health." Spalding was healthy, too, but his wife's suffering gave him a different view. In his letter to the board he stated simply: "Never send another mission over these mountains if you value life and money."

There was something else bothering the missionary couples, something they tried to hide. When they were younger, Henry Spalding had asked Narcissa to marry him, but Narcissa had turned him down. Even though Henry had married Eliza and had a good marriage, the rejection still stung and made it difficult for the couples to work together. But at the Green River rendezvous they had no choice but to work together and find a way to Oregon or go back as failures. At the end of the rendezvous, the fur company caravan would return to St. Louis, the trappers would disappear into the mountains, and the missionaries would be on their own.

The Indians were eager to have them, so eager that Narcissa reported a fight between the Nez Perce women and women of another tribe called the Cayuse, who spoke the Nez Perce language and wanted to get whatever benefits might come with the missionaries. "The Nez Perce women said we were going to live with them & the Cayuses said No, we are going to live with them. The contradiction was so sharp they nearly came to blows."

The Nez Perce were willing to guide the missionaries to their homeland, but they wanted to hunt along the way. Their route followed the spine of the mountains, crossing and recrossing the Continental Divide, which made it impassable for the wagon and extremely difficult for the missionaries' cattle. Another route followed the Snake River through the desolate desert of what is now southern Idaho. This route was difficult, too, but Whitman and Spalding thought they could make it. Two Nez Perce leaders offered to guide the missionaries part of the way, but what the white travelers would do after that was unknown.

Then, like a gift from heaven, a group of fur traders from the British Hudson's Bay Company arrived at the rendezvous. They agreed to escort the missionaries to Fort Walla Walla, a company trading post in what is now eastern Washington. When the missionaries moved their camp closer to the Hudson's Bay men, Thomas McKay, one of the British traders, welcomed them with a much appreciated supper that Narcissa described in mouthwatering detail: "steak (Antelope), boiled ham, biscuit & butter, tea and loaf sugar brought from Walla Walla. This we relished very much for we had seen nothing of the bread kind since the last of May."

The Oregon country was claimed by both the United States and Great Britain, but the real power in Oregon at this time was the Hudson's Bay Company, and the most powerful individual was Dr. John

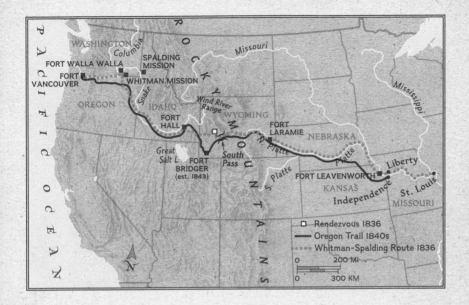

McLoughlin, who ran the company's business from Fort Vancouver on the Columbia River. McLoughlin controlled all the trade in what is now the Pacific Northwest, shipping the valuable furs out of North America, around the tip of South America, and across the Atlantic to Britain. Thomas McKay was McLoughlin's stepson. When he first saw Narcissa and Eliza, McKay realized that the balance of power was about to change.

"There is something that Doctor McLoughlin cannot ship out of the country so easy," said McKay—meaning that these pioneering American women were a force the British could not control. Other American women would follow, and American families would grow in the wilderness where only trappers and Indians had lived before.

And so they did. As the missionaries and British traders headed west on July 18, Narcissa Whitman carried a baby in her womb. She probably didn't know it yet, for the baby would not be born for another eight months. But when this baby, Alice Clarissa Whitman, came into the world at the Whitman Mission on the desolate Columbia Plateau, she became the first American white child born west of the Rockies.

## Historical Note

The story of the four Nez Perce Indians who reached St. Louis in 1831 ignited enthusiasm among Protestant churches to send missionaries west of the Rockies. The first to answer the call were five Methodist missionaries led by Jason Lee who reached Liberty, Missouri, by steamboat in the spring of 1834. They traveled with American fur trader Nathaniel Wyeth to what is now southern Idaho, and then British trader Thomas McKay took them to Fort Walla Walla. From there, they made their way down the Columbia to Fort Vancouver, where John McLoughlin encouraged them to settle in the rich farmland of the Willamette Valley. This would become the primary destination in Oregon for American settlers.

In 1835, Presbyterian missionaries Samuel Parker and Marcus Whitman traveled to the Green River rendezvous. Parker went on to Oregon, but Whitman decided to return to New York to marry Narcissa Prentiss and persuade another missionary couple—the Spaldings—to go West. Parker was supposed to meet Marcus and his party at the 1836 rendezvous and

guide them to Oregon, but he never made it. It is hard to say what the missionaries might have done without the timely arrival of McKay and his Hudson's Bay traders.

Just as Thomas McKay predicted at the 1836 rendezvous, the Whitmans and Spaldings blazed the trail to Oregon for other American families, making a great contribution to the development of the West. Their goal of converting the Indians proved less rewarding. Although the Spaldings had some success among the friendly Nez Perce, the Whitmans struggled with the more warlike Cayuse at their mission near Fort Walla Walla. In 1839, they faced deep personal sorrow when their only child, Alice Clarissa, drowned in the Walla Walla River at the age of two.

Despite these trials, Marcus believed in the importance of the Whitman Mission, if not for the Indians, then for the white settlers who would be arriving soon. The first non-missionary family reached Oregon in 1840, a few more arrived in 1841, and still more came in 1842. In 1843 Marcus helped guide the "Great Migration," which brought some 900 new settlers to

Oregon in the first wagon train to reach the Columbia River.

The Whitman Mission became an important way station on the Oregon Trail. Travelers obtained food, supplies, and medical attention from Marcus, who originally was trained as a doctor. By this time, the Whitmans were the caretakers of four children, and in 1844 they took in a family of seven more whose parents had died on the trail. Narcissa found new happiness caring for all these children, and Marcus proudly realized that his personal efforts had done much to give the United States a strong claim to the Oregon country. A treaty with Great Britain in 1846 gave the United States a vast region, including the present states of Oregon, Washington, Idaho, and parts of Montana and Wyoming.

Then tragedy struck. A measles epidemic in 1847 killed half the Cayuse tribe. Marcus treated both whites and Indians, but the Cayuse blamed him for the deaths. On Monday, November 29, 1847, Cayuse warriors attacked the mission and killed 14 whites, including Marcus and Narcissa Whitman. Even in their deaths, the Whitmans encouraged further settlement. Veteran mountain man Joe Meek persuaded Congress to establish the Oregon Territory to protect the settlers and capture the Whitmans' murderers. By 1850, when five Cayuse Indians were hanged for their parts in the Whitman Massacre, about 12,000 whites lived in Oregon.

*This story is based primarily on the letters and journals of the Whitmans and the Spaldings and on a book written by William Gray, the unmarried man who accompanied them as a "mechanic."*

"The Industrious Miner," by Charles Christian Nahl, portrays the ideal of the early-rising, hardworking California gold miner.

IN THE MEXICAN WAR, THE UNITED STATES WON WHAT BECAME KNOWN AS THE
AMERICAN SOUTHWEST. THE GREATEST PRIZE WAS CALIFORNIA, BUT NO ONE KNEW HOW
VALUABLE IT WAS UNTIL JAMES MARSHALL BUILT A SAWMILL ON THE AMERICAN RIVER.

---

## TALE Nº 4

# I HAVE FOUND IT!

### JAMES MARSHALL DISCOVERS GOLD

---

JAMES MARSHALL EXAMINED THE DITCH that Peter Wimmer and his
Indian crew were digging along the South Fork of the American River.
Called a millrace, the ditch was designed to return water to the river after
turning a big mill wheel; the wheel would power a saw, and the saw would
cut lumber out of trees from the beautiful Coloma Valley that surrounded
them. The lumber would be carried over a rough wagon road and then
floated down the river to John Sutter's fort some 40 miles away.

Sutter needed the lumber for a variety of projects in the growing
settlement he called New Helvetia, or New Switzerland, after the country
where he was born. He was building a big flour mill to provide more food
for the colony, and he had plans to build a town called Sutterville. There
were no usable trees near his fort, so he went into partnership with James
Marshall to build this sawmill in the foothills of the Sierra Nevada. After
several months of steady labor, the mill was nearing completion, but on
this afternoon, Marshall wasn't thinking about lumber.

Down along the bottom of the millrace the hard granite rock was
crumbling. Although he was a carpenter by trade, Marshall knew a little
about geology, and this decomposing granite intrigued him. He motioned

to an Indian and ordered him to run up on the shore and ask a workman named James Brown for a tin plate. Busy cutting wood with a big two-man whipsaw, Brown laid down his end of the saw and remarked out loud, "I wonder what Marshall wants with a tin plate?" Then he headed off to the new log cabin that he and four other men had just moved into that morning.

Brown and the others were members of a religious group called the Mormons. Until that day, they had been living with the family of Peter Wimmer, one of Marshall's non-Mormon employees, and eating meals cooked by Mrs. Wimmer. But they didn't like the way Mrs. Wimmer treated them, so they got permission from Marshall to build their own cabin and cook for themselves. Now James Brown grabbed a tin plate from the new cabin and carried it down to Marshall, who was standing in the millrace.

"This is a curious rock," Marshall said. "I am afraid it will give us trouble." He scooped some sand and gravel from the millrace into the pan and washed it with river water to see if anything interesting floated out. There was nothing, so he chipped off some granite and tried washing

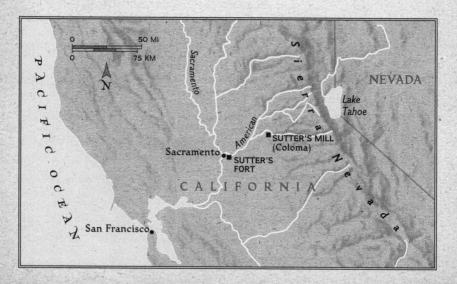

that, too. Nothing. Even so, Marshall suspected the granite contained some kind of mineral, and he believed that somewhere in the rolling, rocky foothills there was gold waiting to be found. He had seen the "blossom," he explained to Brown.

"What do you mean by blossom?" asked the other man.

"Quartz," Marshall replied. ". . . the white flint-like rock so plentiful in the hills." He had read in a book that quartz indicated the presence of gold.

Brown was skeptical. He thought the flintlike rock was just flint, and as for blossoms and gold, well, most folks thought James Marshall was a little strange. Brown called him "notional," meaning he had strange notions or ideas.

James Marshall

At the end of the day, Marshall ordered the men to open the gate and allow the river water to rush though the millrace. They did this every evening, because the river helped clean and deepen the channel. This time the mill boss was hoping for something more than a little help with the labor. "Tonight we will turn on a good head of water," he said, "and tomorrow morning we will come down and see what we can find."

That night, Marshall visited the Mormons at their new cabin. He told Brown and another man named Henry Bigler to get up early and shut the gate. "Throw in a little sawdust, rotten leaves, and dirt and make all tight," he ordered, "and I'll see what's there in the morning."

In the early morning light, the men did as they were told and returned to their own cabin for breakfast. Marshall woke up early, too, and went down to inspect the millrace. The air was clear and cold. Almost a decade later, James Marshall told the story:

> . . . about half past seven . . . I went down as usual, and after shutting off the water from the race I stepped into it, near the lower end, and there, upon the rock, about six inches beneath the

surface of the water, I discovered the gold. I was entirely alone at the time. I picked up one or two pieces and examined them attentively; and having some general knowledge of minerals, I could not call to mind more than two which in any way resembled this—sulphuret of iron [fool's gold], very bright and brittle; and gold, bright, yet malleable; I then tried it between two rocks and found that it could be beaten into a different shape, but not broken.

His heart beating with excitement, Marshall picked up several small flakes of bright metal and dropped them into the crown of his old woolen hat. Then, with his hat held securely in the curve of his arm, he ran up to higher ground where the other men were working in the mill yard. He showed the golden flakes to William Scott, who was working at the carpenter's bench, and shouted, "I have found it!"

"What is it?" Scott asked.

"Gold," Marshall replied.

"Oh! no," said Scott, "that can't be."

Marshall faced the doubter and replied with absolute conviction: "I know it to be nothing else."

Neither Marshall nor any of the other men had ever actually seen gold as it occurs in nature. One of the Mormons, Azariah Smith, had a five-dollar gold piece that he had received as part of his payment for service in the Mexican War, so he took the shiny coin from his pocket and compared it with the golden flakes in James Marshall's hat. The color was different, but that might be because of the other metals that were used in the coin. James Brown took a flake back to the cabin and placed it on the end of an old shovel. Then he tried melting it in the hot fire still burning from breakfast. The fire didn't affect the gold at all. Now Brown was a believer, and he ran back to the other men, shouting, "Gold! Gold!"

Marshall showed the workers where he had found the flakes, and they picked up more, some using jackknives to pry gold from the crevices. When they had enough to fill a small bottle, they entrusted it to James

Sutter's Mill in 1849

Marshall. The boss might be "notional," but they knew he was an honest man. Henry Bigler kept a diary, and according to James Brown, Bigler took the little book from his pocket right there in the millrace and said to his companions, "I must make note of this, for it may be of some importance at some time." Then he wrote the following words:

Sun Monday 24th this day some kind of mettle was discover was found in the tail race that looks like goald.

The fact that Bigler started to write "Sunday" and "was discovered" and then crossed them out has caused confusion over this important diary entry, but January 24, 1848, is considered the official day of the great California gold discovery. Sometime later, when other people tried to claim that they were the first to see the gold, Bigler added to the entry with a different pen: "first discovered by James Martial, the Boss of the Mill."

Around this time, Peter Wimmer arrived and took some bits of gold to his wife, Jane, who was making soap in their cabin. Mrs. Wimmer was from Georgia, where the first American gold rush began in 1828, so she had seen natural gold before. She dropped a piece into the soap kettle to see if the powerful, acidic lye she was using would have any effect on it. Although other metals can be broken down into different parts by acidic chemicals, gold is pure and will not change. The next day, when she took out the hardened soap, the gold was sitting at the bottom of the kettle as bright and shiny as ever. Now Jane Wimmer was a believer, too.

Four days after the discovery, James Marshall rode to John Sutter's fort, carrying some of the gold tied in a rag that he carried in his pocket. By the time he arrived that afternoon, it was pouring rain. Sutter was startled to see his mill boss suddenly appear before him in his office, dripping wet in his buckskin breeches and Mexican serape, obviously excited about something.

"What's the matter?" Sutter asked.

Marshall said he wanted to talk to him where no one else could hear, so the two men went to Sutter's private rooms and locked the door.

"Are we alone?" Marshall asked.

"Yes," Sutter replied.

"I want two bowls of water."

Still wondering what this strange business was about, Sutter rang for one of his servants who brought the water. "Now I want a stick of redwood," said Marshall, when the servant had left, "and some twine and some sheet copper."

"What do you want of all these things, Marshall?" asked Sutter in his accented English.

"I want to make some scales."

Sutter already had a pair of scales in the fort's apothecary shop, so he went to get them himself. When he returned, he forgot to lock the door. Just as Marshall was withdrawing the rag from his pocket, one of Sutter's assistants opened the door and stepped into the room. Marshall quickly thrust the rag back into his pocket. After Sutter sent the man away, Marshall exclaimed, "Now lock the doors; didn't I tell you that we might have listeners?"

The doors safely locked, Marshall pulled out the old rag and showed his partner the glittering flakes. The biggest was the size of a pea, and the smallest would rest on the head of a pin. "I believe this is gold," he said, "but the people at the mill laughed at me, and called me crazy." At least that's how Sutter later remembered it. No one at the mill thought Marshall was crazy, but he was definitely acting a little crazy now—and with good reason.

John Sutter

Sutter examined the flakes and smiled. "Well, it looks so," he said. "We will try it." Again he went to the apothecary shop and brought back nitric acid, which he poured on some of the flakes. Like Mrs. Wimmer's lye, the acid had no effect. Now Marshall wanted some silver, and Sutter had to ask several men at the fort before he came back with a few dollars' worth of silver coins.

Marshall placed equal weights of silver and gold on each side of the scales and then slowly lowered the scales into the two bowls of water. As soon as the side with the gold reached the water, it sank because gold is a denser metal than silver. Now the two men were convinced that this was gold, but they both thought there must be other metals mixed in with it. Sutter had an old set of the *Encyclopedia Americana,* and with the information in the encyclopedia, they tested the flakes until they were certain that there were no other metals at all. "I believe this is the finest kind of gold," Sutter declared.

It was, and the West would never be the same.

[Published at the WIDE WEST OFFICE, 151 Clay Street, San Francisco.]

HOW THE CALIFORNIA MINES ARE WORKED.

## Historical Note

Marshall's discovery set off the California gold rush, the most important single event in the development of the West. At the time of the discovery, California was still officially part of Mexico. Although the fighting in the Mexican War was over, the treaty giving California and other areas of the Southwest to the United States was not signed until February 2, 1848, about a week after the discovery. Both Mexico and Spain had struggled to find people willing to settle in what was then a distant frontier, and it was because of this difficulty that Mexico gave John Sutter broad powers to establish his colony of New Helvetia. On the day that James Marshall found gold, there were probably no more than 14,000 non-Indian people in California, most of them Spanish-speaking. Two years later, the U.S. census counted almost 100,000, and California became the 31st state. In 1860, on the eve of the Civil War, the population was around 380,000, and this does not include all the people who came to California and returned home.

There were various ways to reach California from the East, all of them long and difficult. Some people sailed all the way around the coast of South America and then up to San Francisco; others took a boat to Panama and crossed the isthmus by land to pick up another boat on the other side. Most gold seekers, however, traveled overland, turning old trails into highways through the wilderness. Suddenly, hundreds of thousands of people experienced the West. If things didn't work out in California, or if they just got restless, many of these people moved on to settle other areas. Gold and silver were the driving forces behind these movements, and there were many important mineral discoveries in the years that followed. Mining areas often developed into towns, bringing the white man's civilization to land that had belonged to the Indians a short time before.

The details of the California gold discovery are still uncertain, and there are many puzzling conflicts among the sources. Although various people later claimed to have seen the first gold, most reliable sources agree that it was James Marshall who made the discovery. The description in this story is taken from one of Marshall's own accounts.

Marshall always claimed that the discovery occurred on or around January 19, but he kept no diary. He also said he went to visit John Sutter three or four days after the discovery. The diary of Henry Bigler indicates the discovery occurred on January 24, and John Sutter's diary indicates Marshall visited him "on very important business" on January 28. Azariah Smith kept a diary that placed the discovery sometime in the week of January 23–30. After these diaries were analyzed, the California Legislature established January 24 as the official discovery date, but we will probably never know for sure.

*This story is based on various primary sources that were collected by historian Rodman W. Paul in* The California Gold Discovery *and on the personal reminiscences of John Sutter as told to 19th-century historian Hubert Howe Bancroft. In interpreting the conflicting sources, I have generally followed the excellent biography of James Marshall by Theressa Gay.*

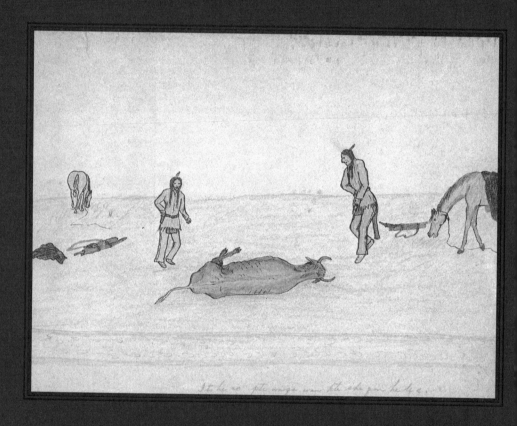

A Lakota named Black Horse, whose grandfather participated in
the Grattan fight, portrays the killing of the cow along the Oregon Trail
that began the unfortunate chain of events recounted in this tale.

WITH THE DISCOVERY OF GOLD IN CALIFORNIA, THE MORMON MIGRATION TO UTAH, AND CONTINUING EMIGRATION TO OREGON, TENS OF THOUSANDS OF WAGON WHEELS ROLLED ACROSS INDIAN LANDS.

## TALE № 5

# BLOOD ON THE TRAIL

### THE GRATTAN FIGHT

ON A HOT AUGUST AFTERNOON IN 1854, an old, lame cow was shot along the Oregon Trail about eight miles east of Fort Laramie. According to some reports, the cow had lagged behind a wagon train, and when its owner tried to drive it forward, the animal bolted into an Indian village. Others claimed the cow was left to die on the trail. The owner insisted the cow was taken by force and that he himself had barely escaped with his life. One fact is clear: The cow was killed by a Lakota warrior called High Forehead, who shared the meat with his hungry friends.

High Forehead was one of several thousand Lakota and Cheyenne camping near Fort Laramie, waiting for the annual payment of food and supplies that the U.S. government had promised them in a treaty three years earlier. In return for these payments, the Indians promised not to bother white people traveling along the trail. The Indians called the trail the Holy Road, because they considered their promise to be sacred.

That year, the government agent who was supposed to hand out the food and supplies was late. So the precious goods lay locked in the Gratiot Houses, a trading post about five miles outside the fort, while the Indians grew hungrier and more frustrated with every passing day. Their ponies ate what little grass was left along the trail, and the warriors ranged farther and farther from camp to find meat for their families. Even so, the death of the cow was a violation of the treaty, and the Indians were expected to pay for the loss.

The chief of the village where High Forehead and his friends ate the cow was called Conquering Bear. He had signed the treaty, and the whites considered him chief of all Lakota. In reality, he was a "paper chief" whose authority existed only on the paper of the treaty. The Lakota never had a single chief; they had many leaders, and each warrior followed a leader he respected.

The Lakota—whom the whites called the Teton Sioux—were the largest tribe on the Plains at this time, some 15,000 strong. They were divided into seven bands, or "council fires," each a powerful force in its own right. Conquering Bear was one of two principal chiefs of a band called the Brule, who had always kept the peace. High Forehead belonged to another band called the Miniconjou, who had skirmished with whites

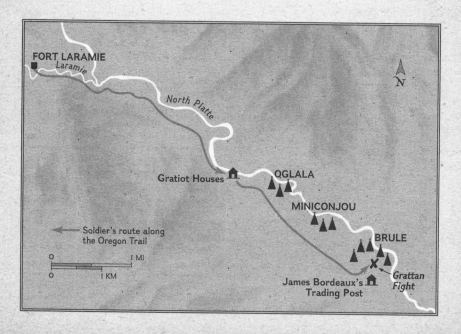

the year before and still held bad feelings toward them. He was a guest in Conquering Bear's village, and this made the situation complicated. Just as the whites had laws and customs, so did the Lakota.

On the afternoon of August 18, Conquering Bear rode into Fort Laramie to report the incident to the commanding officer, Second Lieutenant Hugh Fleming, who had graduated from West Point just two years earlier. The captain of the wagon train that had lost the cow reported the incident around the same time. Fleming and Conquering Bear discussed the situation through an interpreter named Auguste Lucien, who was angry at the Indians for stealing two of his own animals just a few days earlier. Communication was always difficult in early contacts between Indians and whites, but Lucien's attitude made it even more difficult.

The Bear, as Fleming called him, offered a horse in payment for the cow. This was a generous offer, because a horse was worth much more than a cow on the frontier, but the cow's owner refused to accept it. He was a Mormon convert from Denmark, where cows and dairy products were the heart of the economy. So perhaps he didn't understand that he was being offered something more valuable. Perhaps he was just being difficult. Perhaps he didn't speak enough English to understand the offer at all.

Lieutenant Fleming asked the Bear to hand over High Forehead, promising that he would be kept safe at the fort until the agent arrived. According to the treaty, the agent could hold back some of the food and supplies as a punishment for violations, and Fleming figured he would let the agent decide what was fair. The lieutenant thought Conquering Bear promised to give up High Forehead, but it seems more likely that the chief said something like "I will try to give you High Forehead." The difference between a promise and a promise to try was easily lost in translation.

Conquering Bear returned to his camp and met with his trusted advisers. High Forehead refused to go into the fort, and because he was a visitor, Conquering Bear could not force him to go. Instead, the Bear sent a respected younger chief of the Oglala band, who were camping just up the river. This chief's Lakota name is usually translated as Man Afraid of His Horses, but the true meaning of the name is that he was so powerful that just the sight of his horses made other people afraid. Again, so much is lost in translation. We'll just call him Man.

Man arrived at Fort Laramie on the afternoon of August 19, in the middle of a whirling windstorm, just in time to watch preparations for a military expedition. Later, through a translator, he described what he saw:

> The young Officer then went to the Soldiers House and the next thing I saw was a wagon go over to the adobe Fort and next saw the Soldiers draw a cannon out of the Fort. I went out of the store and stood by the cannon, saw the Soldiers taking a great many things out of the house then saw them clean out the cannon prepairing to load it. The Officer then went to the Store and talked very loud.

The loud-talking officer was John L. Grattan. He was 24, a year younger than Fleming, and he was only a brevet second lieutenant, which was a temporary rank until a vacancy opened up that would allow him to have a real officer's commission. Brash, brave, and eager to prove himself, he had obtained permission from Lieutenant Fleming to try to take High Forehead. If the Indian refused to come, Grattan was supposed to use his judgment and fight only if he thought he could win. Although Fleming ordered Grattan to take 20 men, he took 30, including the interpreter Auguste Lucien. Most of the men rode in the wagon, pulled by mules, and mules also pulled two cannons. Accompanied by Man and a white civilian named Obridge Allen, the expedition left the fort in mid-afternoon and headed down the Oregon Trail.

Before leaving the fort, Auguste Lucien had told Man that he feared the Indians might kill him because of the bad feelings between them. To calm his nerves, Lucien began drinking whiskey at the fort and continued drinking along the way. The soldiers in the wagon were drinking, too.

Man Afraid of His Horses (third from left) poses with other Sioux and Cheyenne leaders at Fort Laramie in 1868, where they negotiated a new treaty with the U.S. government.

Although some reports suggest Lieutenant Grattan was drunk, Obridge Allen and Man both said they never saw the officer drink along the road.

After traveling for more than an hour, the expedition stopped to rest at the Gratiot Houses, where the food and supplies for the Indians were still locked up. Some Indians were visiting the post, and Lucien began to taunt them, riding his horse up and down, brandishing his pistol in the air. "You do not believe what you are told," he shouted, "but the soldiers will give you a new set of ears." Lucien got more whiskey at the trading post, but Lieutenant Grattan took the bottle away from him and smashed it against his saddle.

Beyond the Gratiot Houses, the trail climbed along the sandstone bluffs of the North Platte River Valley, giving Grattan a good view of the

Lakota camps—at least 600 lodges stretching for some three miles along the river. "Do you see how many lodges there are?" asked Obridge Allen.

"Yes, but I don't care how many there are; with thirty men I can whip all the Indians this side of the Missouri," Grattan boasted. Farther down the trail, Grattan ordered his men to halt and load their weapons. "Men," he said, "I don't believe we shall have a fight; but I hope to God we may have one."

By late afternoon, the expedition arrived at another trading post, which was owned by a Frenchman named James Bordeaux, who was married to a Lakota woman and who had many Indians camping near his post. Again the drunken Lucien stirred up trouble, riding back and forth in front of the Indians, shouting, "The Sioux are all women! I will have you killed and eat your hearts before sundown!" Bordeaux urged Grattan to quiet the interpreter, but by now Lucien was too drunk to control.

James Bordeaux

The Brule camp was only 300 yards away from Bordeaux's trading post, and Conquering Bear soon arrived to discuss the situation. He had a fair interpreter in James Bordeaux, but when Grattan demanded that he hand over High Forehead, the Bear stalled for time. "I must go and put on my dress-coat before I give an answer," he said. He returned to his lodge and came back with the coat, probably part of the general's uniform that had been given to him as a present when he signed the treaty promising peace along the trail. A Lakota messenger announced that High Forehead refused to give himself up. Grattan demanded him anyway, and the Bear explained that it was the custom of his people to ask four times before taking action. Finally, he suggested that Grattan go to High Forehead's lodge himself and see what the warrior had to say.

James Bordeaux warned Lieutenant Grattan that it would be foolish to enter the Indian village, but the officer was determined. "I have two revolvers with twelve shots," he said.

"Take them out of your holsters and be ready," Bordeaux replied.

As the soldiers marched toward the Brule camp, Conquering Bear rode double on the horse of Auguste Lucien. Once inside the camp, Grattan ordered his men to line up on either side of the two cannons while he held another long conference with the Lakota leaders. James Bordeaux was afraid to enter the camp, so he watched from his trading post as the drunken Auguste Lucien—still hostile toward the Indians—acted as interpreter.

High Forehead stood defiantly at the door of his lodge with five other Miniconjou warriors, all of them stripped for battle. He complained about the way the whites had treated his people and challenged Grattan to fight him man to man to the death. Conquering Bear and Man tried to persuade High Forehead to give himself up, but he refused. They also tried to persuade Lieutenant Grattan to "cover up" the trouble until the Indian agent arrived. The Bear offered a valuable mule instead of a horse if Grattan would just let the agent deal with it. But Grattan was as stubborn as High Forehead. "To day the Soldiers have made me ashamed," said Conquering Bear. "I was made Chief by the Whites and to day you come to my village and plant your big guns."

As the men talked, young Oglala warriors sneaked into the Brule camp and began to ride their horses up and down as if preparing for battle. Brule warriors rode their horses down a dry creek bed and hid behind the wild roses and thick brush, applying war paint and setting war bonnets on their heads. Lieutenant Grattan saw at least some of this activity, but either he did not take it seriously or he thought the warriors were riding off because they were afraid of his guns. The Brule women knew better; they gathered their children and fled toward the river.

The Indian leaders did not trust Lucien's translation, and twice Man left the meeting to go and ask James Bordeaux to come and interpret. "My friend, come on," he said. "The interpreter is going to get us into a fight." Bordeaux mounted Obridge Allen's horse, but the stirrups were too long for him, and he turned back. Strange as it may sound, that was his explanation. When Man came a second time, Bordeaux mounted the horse again and followed him, but it was too late.

Frustrated and angry, Lieutenant Grattan broke off the conversation and barked an order the Indians didn't understand. Suddenly, shots rang out and an Indian fell to the ground. James Bordeaux heard the chiefs shouting at their warriors not to fight. The soldiers had drawn Lakota blood, one chief reasoned, and perhaps that was enough to protect the soldiers' honor. Perhaps they would leave. But they didn't leave. Grattan ordered his men to fire a full volley, and Conquering Bear—paper chief of the Lakota—fell mortally wounded in front of his own lodge.

Now there was no holding back. The warriors attacked, arrows whizzing through the air, striking the soldiers with deadly accuracy. Lieutenant Grattan fired one of his cannons uselessly above the Indian lodges before he fell in a shower of arrows. The men scattered in terror, some running for their lives, others loading their wounded comrades into the wagon and heading for the trail.

Few Indians had guns, so the soldiers' musket balls kept them at a distance for a time, but there were too few soldiers and too many Indians. In a flat area along the trail, the warriors finished off the soldiers with a flurry of arrows, lances, and tomahawks. One soldier made it back to the fort, only to die of his wounds before he could tell the story. According to Lakota tradition, Auguste Lucien was the last to die, begging and pleading for his life. Lieutenant John Grattan was found dead beside the cannons with two dozen arrows in his body. His face was so mutilated that he could be identified only by his pocket watch.

Excited by the battle, the Lakota warriors wanted to attack Fort Laramie, but James Bordeaux talked them out of it. The Great Father in

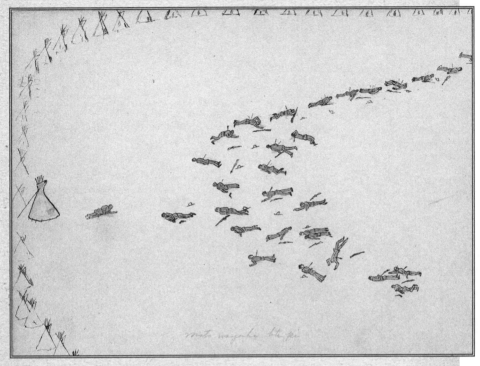

This colored-pencil drawing by Black Horse shows dead soldiers and Conquering Bear mortally wounded in front of his lodge.

Washington would see that the soldiers were partly at fault, he told them, and he would forgive the warriors for the battle. But he would never forgive an attack on the fort. Instead, the warriors took what they wanted from Bordeaux's trading post, and the next morning they broke into the storehouse at the Gratiot Houses and took the food and supplies that the agent was supposed to give them. Within a few days, they scattered into the hills and plains.

The Great Father did not forgive them for the battle, and the Grattan fight began a quarter century of warfare between the Lakota and the United States—over an old, lame cow.

## Historical Note

In the 19th century, the Sioux were the largest and most powerful Indian nation west of the Mississippi River. By this time, the seven original Sioux tribes had formed three cultural groups. The Santee Sioux were farmers who lived in permanent villages in what is now southern Minnesota. The Yankton Sioux lived farther west and practiced a combination of farming and hunting. Today, the Santee and Yankton Sioux are often called the Dakota, which is the name they call themselves in the Siouan language. The Teton Sioux, or Lakota, lived even farther west. They depended almost entirely on the buffalo, following the great herds across the northern Plains in what is now the Dakotas, Nebraska, Montana, and Wyoming.

On their voyage up the Missouri River in 1804, Lewis and Clark encountered both Yankton and Teton Sioux. Though there were some minor conflicts in later years, relations between the United States and the Sioux were generally peaceful until 1854. In 1851, after the gold rush dramatically increased traffic along the Oregon-California Trail, a great conference was held near Fort Laramie with representatives of many Plains tribes attending. In the Treaty of Fort Laramie, the Plains were divided into areas for each tribe, the Indians promised not to fight among themselves, and— most important—they recognized "the right of the United States Government to establish roads, military and other posts" and promised to pay for any losses of the whites or other Indians. In return, the Indians were supposed to receive $50,000 worth of food and supplies every year for 50 years. Congress reduced the period to 15 years and raised the amount to $70,000, but the Indians never agreed to it.

The deaths of Lieutenant Grattan and his men were the first serious breakdown of the treaty, ending the long peace between the Sioux and the United States. A military investigation gathered testimony from many key witnesses shortly after the events. Most accounts are remarkably consistent, and it seems clear that Lieutenant Grattan went looking for a fight. Senator Thomas Hart Benton, a great supporter of western expansion, denounced the Army for destroying 50 years of peace with the Sioux by "sending our school-house officers and pot-house soldiers to treat the Indians as beasts and dogs." (The term "pot-house soldiers" was meant to suggest that the soldiers were as young and inexperienced as their officers, like young plants grown in what we would call a greenhouse.)

The Army refused to accept the results of its own investigation and instead decided to punish the Lakota. On September 3, 1855, 700 U.S. troops under General William S. Harney attacked a Brule village near Ash Hollow, Nebraska, killing approximately 100 Indians and capturing 70 more. The attack quieted Lakota resistance for a decade, but the damage had been done. The Lakota would prove to be a powerful foe of U.S. expansion and travel across the Plains.

*This story is based on testimony collected by the Army and sent to the House of Representatives in 1855 and the Senate in 1856. Among these accounts are testimonies from James Bordeaux, Obridge Allen, Lieutenant Fleming, and two different investigating officers. I have also used the account given by Man Afraid of His Horses shortly after the battle. All of these accounts are used and quoted extensively in "The Grattan Massacre" by Lloyd E. McCann.*

"First Ride," by Charles Hargens, captures the excitement as the first
Pony Express rider leaves St. Joseph, Missouri, on April 3, 1860.

IN EARLY 1860, IT TOOK THREE WEEKS FOR MAIL TO REACH CALIFORNIA FROM THE EASTERN UNITED STATES. A VISIONARY BUSINESSMAN NAMED WILLIAM H. RUSSELL CLAIMED HIS COMPANY COULD DELIVER IT IN TEN DAYS.

## TALE Nº 6

# THEY'RE OFF!

## FIRST RIDE OF THE PONY EXPRESS

THE STREETS OF ST. JOSEPH looked like the Fourth of July, with American flags flying and red, white, and blue bunting decorating the stores and offices of the downtown area. The crowd began to gather in the late afternoon, eagerly awaiting a glimpse of history: the first ride of the Pony Express to California. It was Tuesday, April 3, 1860.

1860

A little before 5:00 p.m.—when the train carrying letters from the East was scheduled to arrive—a "fine bay mare" was led out of the Pike's Peak Stables. She was the first in a long parade of horses that would carry the mail to California. As her keeper walked the mare around to warm her up, some of the onlookers plucked hairs from her tail as souvenirs— so many hairs that a local paper reported "the little pony was almost robbed of its tail." The horse didn't like that much, so her keeper led her back into the stables.

That disappointed the crowd, but the real disappointment came when they found out that the eastern train would be late. A brass band tried to entertain them, but the people of St. Joseph weren't interested in brass bands on this particular afternoon. They wanted to see that horse and rider take off carrying the mail.

At this time, mail to California was carried by stagecoach on a long curving route from St. Louis, Missouri, or Memphis, Tennessee, to Fort Smith, Arkansas, south to El Paso, Texas, and on to southern California, before heading north to Sacramento and San Francisco. Or it was carried by steamship from New York to Panama, by railroad across the isthmus, and then picked up by another boat on the Pacific side that took it on to San Francisco. Whether by land or sea, the journey took three weeks or more, but now the Pony Express promised to carry mail from St. Joseph to San Francisco in just ten days. It was a bold promise, and on this first day the company was already behind schedule.

Despite the delay, the officials of the town and the express company carried on with their ceremony and speeches. St. Joseph mayor M. Jeff Thompson captured the spirit and excitement of the day, predicting that the Pony Express was only the forerunner of a railroad to California that would transform the West:

> I say that the wilderness which lies between us and that El Dorado will soon blossom as the rose. Cities will spring into existence where the Indians and buffalo now hold possession. The dry and useless desert will be made to yield abundant crops. Mountains will be tunnelled, streams bridged, and the iron monster which has become Mankind's slave will ply between our confines and those far distant shores. As the Indian vanishes, the white man takes his place. Commercial activity will replace the teepee and the campfire. Schools and colleges will span the continent.

William H. Russell—the driving force behind the Pony Express—and one of his partners, Alexander Majors, made similar speeches. But all the speeches in the world couldn't get the mail to California until the mail arrived from the East.

Finally, around 7:00 p.m., a little steam locomotive called the Missouri screeched into the station pulling a single car. The train had just set a company speed record, flying along the tracks at full throttle from

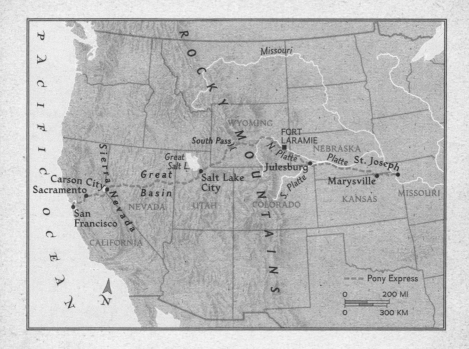

the eastern Missouri city of Palmyra. In the passenger car was a special messenger carrying 49 letters, 5 telegrams, and some newspapers, sent from Washington, D.C., New York, and perhaps some other cities along the way. The messenger had missed his connection in Detroit—that's why he was late—but the little locomotive had made up some of the time.

The messenger carried the mail to the starting point, most likely outside the stables or just up Penn Street at the offices of the Central Overland California & Pike's Peak Express Company, which operated the Pony Express. There the precious papers were wrapped in oiled silk to protect them from rain, snow, and swollen rivers. The mail was then placed into a special leather saddlebag called a *mochilla*, designed to be thrown quickly over the horse's back.

At 7:15 p.m. a brass cannon boomed, and the first rider took off into the gathering darkness, cheered on by the boisterous crowd. We don't know for sure who this first rider was, and there have been many arguments over the years about his identity. One local paper reported it was "a Mr. Richardson, formerly a sailor, and a man accustomed to every description of hardship." Other eyewitnesses reported it was Johnny Fry, a small, handsome young man who lived just south of town.

Years later, an old man named Billy Richardson, who was nine years old in April 1860, claimed that he was "just nosing around at the Pony Express barn," with his own little pony. "When the cannon was fired . . . an agent of the express company threw the mail on my pony just for a joke." According to Richardson, he rode with the mail down to the Missouri River, just a short dash from the starting point, and gave it to Johnny Fry. Maybe that's the way it really happened, and that might explain the confusion with "Mr. Richardson," although how a newspaper reporter could think nine-year-old Billy Richardson was a tough sailor is anybody's guess.

At the riverbank, the first rider guided his horse onto a waiting ferry that carried them across to the Kansas side, where another crowd cheered as horse and rider rode west into the warm spring night. Pushing hard, the rider made up some of the lost time, quickly changing horses at several stops along the way. Sometime after midnight, he handed the mailbag to 16-year-old Don Rising, who leaped onto his own horse and thundered off into the darkness. By 8:15 that morning, Don was in Marysville, Kansas, 140 miles from St. Joseph. The westbound mail was well on its way.

The eastbound mail began its journey in San Francisco, on the afternoon of the same day the westbound mail left St. Joseph. Thousands of

Poster advertising the
Pony Express

people converged on the city to watch the festivities. Businesses closed, and the main streets were decorated with arches of flowers. There were brass bands, booming cannons, and speeches.

At 4:00 p.m. local time, in front of the offices of the *Alta Telegraph* newspaper, a mochilla carrying 85 letters was swung onto "a clean-limbed, hardy little nankeen-colored pony" with two little American flags decorating the bridle. (The word "nankeen" referred to a brownish yellow cloth imported from China.) A rider named James Randall mounted from the wrong side of the pony and sped down the street to the waterfront, where a steamboat waited to carry the mail to Sacramento. Randall was not a real Pony Express rider, but most of the crowd didn't know the difference.

Richard Egan carried the first westbound mail out of Salt Lake City. His father carried the eastbound mail into the city.

Randall and the little pony were just for show, and they probably didn't even travel on the boat. The real journey began when the steamer reached Sacramento around 2:45 a.m. in the midst of a driving rainstorm. There was no crowd to watch as a real Pony Express rider, William Hamilton, swung the saddlebags onto his horse and rode into the night. Following a trail along the American River, he headed east in the rainy darkness, making good time despite the bad conditions. After several changes of horses, he reached a station in the foothills of the Sierra Nevada and handed the mail to Warren Upson. Warren's father was the editor of the *Sacramento Union,* an important paper in the state capital, and Warren was an impressive young man in his own right.

Warren's ride began around 7:45 a.m. The trail ahead of him over the mountains, uphill, rocky, and treacherous, was covered in such heavy snow that the stage line to Carson City, Nevada—which hadn't missed a run in three years—was unable to cross. At a relay station called Strawberry, the division superintendent met the young rider with a string of mules to help break a trail through the newly fallen, drifting snow. Even so, Warren had to dismount in places to lead his horse, and a bone-chilling arctic wind howled down on them as they struggled toward the summit of the massive granite mountain wall that stood as the greatest natural obstacle on the entire line of the Pony Express.

Just as he reached the summit, Warren passed a group of men crossing with mules from the other side of the mountains. "The storm grew fiercer and fiercer as we went on," reported one of the travelers. "The flakes of snow and hail were blowing into our faces with such power that they stung like needles, and nearly blinded us. . . . On the very summit, we met a lonely rider dashing along at a tremendous rate. We wondered what could possibly induce him to go on through that gale, and thought it must be some important business. It was the Pony Express."

Working his way down the steep and narrow trail of the eastern slope, Warren rode out of the snowstorm as he reached the lower elevations.

Warren Upson crossed the Sierra Nevada in the midst of a driving snowstorm.

Some say he passed the mail on at the first Nevada station, others that he rode all the way to Carson City. Either way, Warren Upson's crossing of the snow-covered Sierra Nevada proved the mail could go through under the most treacherous conditions.

From Carson City to Salt Lake City, the Pony Express stations stood like lonely outposts of white civilization in a harsh land populated by Indians. Later there would be trouble with the Indians along this route, but on this first run the mail moved steadily onward under blue skies and good, dry trail conditions. At 11:45 p.m. on Saturday, April 7, Howard Egan—an older man who was a district superintendent rather than a regular rider—galloped into Salt Lake City and passed the mail on to another rider outside the Pony Express office. In spite of the snowstorm in the Sierra Nevada, the eastbound express was well ahead of schedule.

Salt Lake City was the only large settlement between Carson City and St. Joseph, so it was a natural halfway point along the route. It was closer to the western end, however, and the mail from St. Joseph was lagging behind schedule due to bad weather. The rider did not arrive until April 9. Sometime on the day before, the eastbound and westbound riders passed along the trail. Did they tip their hats and shout a word of greeting? Did they stop for a moment and shake hands or share a few words? Or did they simply thunder onward toward the next station? We'll never know, but at that moment, the sprawling western territory had been connected as it had never been connected before.

East of South Pass the road was better, carved out by the wagon wheels of the Mormons and the emigrants to Oregon and California. Spring rains made the going rough in places, however, and the greatest danger came at Julesburg, Colorado, where the eastbound rider crossed the rain-swollen Platte River. A crowd watched from the opposite bank as the rider bravely rode his horse into the rushing river. Suddenly, the horse lost its footing and was swept downstream into quicksand. Thinking quickly, the rider grabbed the mochilla and waded across to the opposite shore,

The eastbound and westbound riders meet on the trail somewhere east of Salt Lake City in this illustration from John F. Clampitt's *Echoes from the Rocky Mountains,* first published in 1880.

borrowed a horse from an onlooker, and continued on his way to the cheers of the crowd. The people of Julesburg pulled the horse out of the river.

At 5:00 p.m. on April 13, Johnny Fry—riding the last leg of the eastward journey—arrived at the Pony Express offices in St. Joseph and carried the mochilla inside. There were no standard time zones in those days, but the local time in St. Joseph was about two hours later than San Francisco time. The well-worn leather saddlebags had made a journey of almost 2,000 miles in 9 days and 23 hours. Again the people of St. Joseph took to the streets in celebration. Militiamen fired their muskets into the air, the cannon boomed, and bonfires and fireworks lit the sky.

The westbound mail was slower, but not by much. A little before 5:30 p.m. on April 13, William Hamilton—the same man who had carried the mail out of Sacramento—reached Sutter's Fort just outside the city. He found a welcoming committee of 95 mounted horsemen in a double line who escorted him and his mustang pony into the California capital, where flags flew from public buildings and along the major streets. Church bells rang and cannons fired. Men, women, and children lined the streets and watched from porches and rooftops, cheering and waving their hats and handkerchiefs.

At the Pony Express office, the mochilla was opened and the Sacramento mail quickly removed. Then Hamilton remounted his mustang and headed to the riverfront, where he boarded a ferry bound for San Francisco. At 12:38 a.m. the boat arrived at the dock, greeted by fire bells, skyrockets, and bonfires. As they left the ferry, horse and rider found themselves swept up into the center of a parade, with a band and four fire companies in the lead and hordes of citizens walking or riding behind. The band played "See, the Conquering Hero Comes" as they marched to the *Alta Telegraph* office, where the eastward journey had begun ten days and nine hours earlier. By this time it was about one in the morning. Instead of long speeches, the crowd gave three last cheers for the Pony Express and went home to bed.

Or at least the older folks went home. The young boys stayed out all night, celebrating this great moment, feeling the energy and excitement in the San Francisco air—and feeling much closer than they had ever felt before to their fellow Americans in the East.

The Pony Express carried news of Abraham Lincoln's election in record time.

## Historical Note

The California gold rush created a pressing need for communication between the eastern and western United States. By 1860, the year the Pony Express began, there were 380,000 people in California, with smaller but substantial settlements in the mining regions of western Nevada, the fertile Willamette Valley of Oregon, the Mormon enclaves around Salt Lake City, and the new mines of Colorado. All of these people wanted to know what was happening in the East. At the same time, Easterners were eager for news from the West.

The first regular mail service to California was by steamboat from New York to San Francisco with a land crossing at the isthmus of Panama. Even after a railroad was built across the isthmus in 1855, mail on this route took a little more than three weeks. The people of California demanded faster service, and they believed the fastest service would be overland. In 1857, the United States awarded a mail contract to the Overland Mail Company, which offered passenger and mail service by stagecoach out of St. Louis and Memphis on a long, sweeping route through the Southwest. This took an average of 21 to 23 days, about the same as the ocean route. Four other mail routes developed over the next two years, including one over the central route later used by the Pony Express. The federal government favored the southern route and the Overland Mail. President James Buchanan was a personal friend of Overland Mail president John Butterfield.

In 1859, the U.S. postmaster general effectively wiped out competition to the Overland Mail. This alarmed Northerners who strongly favored the central route, which would keep the rich mines of California, Nevada, and Colorado connected to the North in the event of war. To prove the superiority of the central route, the freighting company of Russell, Majors, and Waddell established a new company called the Central Overland California & Pike's Peak Express Company, which operated the Pony Express. In an amazing feat of organization, it put the company and the route together in about 60 days, using some stations from earlier routes, building new stations, buying horses, hiring riders and station keepers, and sending out supplies to keep these men alive and working.

The Pony Express was remarkably successful in delivering mail and news on time. Although it was closed for a while due to Indian troubles and had problems with winter weather, it proved once and for all that the central route could work. Unfortunately, it was a disaster financially. Sending mail by Pony Express was expensive: $5.00 in gold for a letter weighing up to a half ounce. Though this was later reduced, the number of items sent was never enough to pay expenses. Even so, the Pony Express continued to operate until October 26, 1861, when a telegraph line was completed from St. Joseph to San Francisco. It was the success of the Pony Express along the central route that pushed the telegraph project forward. By the end of the decade a railroad would be completed along almost the same line, the iron horse following the pony.

*The story of the first ride is full of contradictions that can never be settled completely. I have used newspaper articles and unpublished sources supplied to me by the St. Joseph Museum, a historical resource study done for the National Park Service, and information from several books written on the Pony Express that contain extensive quotes from original sources.*

Chief engineers Samuel Montague (left foreground) of the Central Pacific and Grenville Dodge (right foreground) of the Union Pacific shake hands after the golden spike ceremony in this classic photograph by Andrew J. Russell.

IN 1862, PRESIDENT ABRAHAM LINCOLN AUTHORIZED TWO RAILROAD COMPANIES TO BUILD TRACKS ACROSS THE WESTERN UNITED STATES. SEVEN YEARS LATER THEY MET IN A LONELY UTAH BASIN.

## TALE № 7

# A RAILROAD TO THE MOON

### COMPLETION OF THE TRANSCONTINENTAL RAILROAD

ON A RAINY FRIDAY MORNING, May 7, 1869, the Central Pacific steam locomotive Jupiter rolled into a circular, sagebrush-covered valley in northern Utah. Behind the little engine was its "tender," or coal car, a supply car, and a special passenger car carrying Leland Stanford, former governor of California and president of the Central Pacific Railroad, along with other dignitaries and friends. They had rushed over the rails to this lonely place to take part in a ceremony that newspapers called second only to the signing of the Declaration of Independence: the completion of the first transcontinental railroad. But something was wrong.

Stepping out of the car, Stanford and the others looked ahead to where the Central Pacific rails ended. There was a sandy gap long enough for several sets of rails, then the Union Pacific rails began, heading toward the Northeast. This was as it should be, but the rest of the scene was strangely empty: two or three tents, a few dangerous-looking characters hanging around, and two telegraph operators, one at the end of each railroad line. Where were the crowds, they wondered, and the workmen? And most important, where was the train from the East carrying the representatives of the Union Pacific Railroad?

The ceremony was scheduled for the next day, Saturday, May 8, and the nation was eagerly waiting for it to begin. Parades were planned in San Francisco and Sacramento, and eastern cities had festivities planned as well. Thirty-one years earlier, when the citizens of Dubuque, Iowa, asked Congress to build a western railroad, they were told they might as well ask "to build a railroad to the moon." Now the Central Pacific and Union Pacific had built that railroad with an awesome display of energy and ingenuity. Yet on this cold, rainy Friday, in a desolate saucer-shaped basin surrounded by eroded mountains—a place called Promontory Summit—it looked like they really had built a railroad to the moon.

Neither telegraph operator could explain the situation, so the Union Pacific man tapped out a question and sent it over the wires. There was trouble down the tracks, signaled an operator to the east. The Union Pacific train could not arrive until Monday. This was bad news; the Central Pacific operator—sitting just to the southwest of the UP man—had the unpleasant duty of tapping out a message from Stanford to event organizers in California, informing them of the delay. It was too late to stop the celebrations, they decided, so they would hold them as planned. But they'd do their best to keep the party going until Monday.

Melting snow and hard spring rains had wiped out part of a bridge at

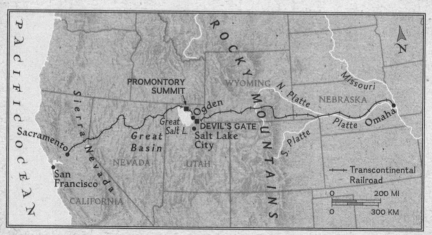

Devil's Gate in the Wasatch Mountains of eastern Utah. As the two railroads raced for completion, each greedily trying to gain the government land and money that went with every mile of track, bridges were built quickly and poorly. The special train carrying Union Pacific vice president Thomas Durant and other dignitaries would have to wait until the bridge was repaired.

Leland Stanford

But that was only part of the story. Durant's train had been stopped in Wyoming by more than 300 angry men who worked for a company that cut railroad ties for the Union Pacific. The men hadn't been paid in months, and they refused to let the train leave—or other trains pass—until they received $200,000. Several UP leaders—including those who had to bail him out—believed that Durant himself organized the attack because he owned stock in the tie-cutting company, and this was the only way he could get more money out of the Union Pacific. The train was allowed to move on after the men received a payment of $50,000, but if Durant did plan the attack, he didn't plan for the washed-out bridge.

So it was that on Saturday, May 8, while Stanford and his party did their best to amuse themselves and Durant's party stewed in their car behind the broken bridge, San Francisco and Sacramento held huge parades and celebrations. "By nine o'clock the city was crowded in all the principal streets," reported the *Sacramento Union*, "with the largest, most orderly and eager number of people ever collected here at one time—and still they came, from farms, roads, river, in boats, cars, and every conceivable style of conveyance, till the sidewalks . . . were too small to hold the throng." The celebration lasted late into the night, with booming cannons ringing bells, blaring train whistles, stirring speeches, and inspiring banners—all for a magical moment that had not yet happened.

●　●　●

AFTER A RAINY WEEKEND, the sun rose in clear skies over Promontory on Monday, May 10. Union Pacific laborers had worked through the night to complete a side track for a station; when a Central Pacific construction train arrived in the early morning carrying workers to build their own siding, they saw that they had been beaten in this last little race. It didn't matter much. The station at Promontory was hardly a prize, so the workers mingled in the early morning light. Local Mormon farmers began to arrive, and more tents sprang up; by noon there would

Thomas C. Durant

be 16, some of them advertising rotgut whiskey with names like Red Cloud, Red Jacket, and Blue Run. High above on a telegraph pole, an American flag fluttered in the breeze.

At 8:20 a.m., a Union Pacific train arrived from Ogden, Utah, the nearest station to the east. It carried sightseers and three photographers, each with his own camera. Stanford had brought a photographer, too, and the four men started taking photos of this historic event, vying for angles and position, sometimes catching each other in their shots. Photography was a new technology. The big, bulky cameras were difficult to maneuver, and the slow-exposing photographic plates required the subjects to stand perfectly still for a clear picture.

Around 10 o'clock, the long-awaited train carrying Durant and other Union Pacific officials arrived. Stanford and his party immediately went over to meet them in Durant's luxurious Pullman car, all beautiful wood and brass. Durant looked luxurious himself, "with a black velvet coat and gay neck-tie . . . gorgeously gotten up," according to a friend of Stanford. Durant may have looked good, but he didn't feel good. He was suffering from a splitting headache, caused, perhaps, by too much stress along the way or by too much champagne the night before. He stayed in his Pullman car while the other Union Pacific men stepped outside for a photograph.

Durant's train carried some U.S. Army officers and their wives on their way to San Francisco, and another train arrived later with the regular soldiers and regimental band. They had all been stranded with Durant behind the washed-out bridge, and he had graciously offered his luxurious car to the ladies. In between, another train from Ogden brought reporters, a Mormon band, and Mormon leaders, some with their wives. One count found 21 women out of 500 or 600 people that day, but on the remote frontier, the presence of women always made the party a little more special.

As Chinese workers from the Central Pacific finished the final stretch of track—leaving room for two last rails and one last tie—the wood-burning engine Jupiter pulled Stanford's train forward. Durant's train, pulled by coal-burning engine No. 119, stood facing Jupiter with a short stretch of track between them. Reporters wrote that Jupiter was decorated with colorful ribbons, little American flags, and California evergreens, but none of these decorations can be seen in the photographs taken that day. Most reporters wrote their stories before the ceremony, so maybe these decorations were planned but never carried out.

A beautiful railroad tie of polished laurel wood was taken from Stanford's train and laid carefully on the ground beside the final section of track. Two gangs of workers, blue-jacketed Chinese from the Central Pacific and burly Irishmen from the Union Pacific, carried the last two heavy iron rails forward and set them into place. The workers, or their foremen, drove some of the spikes for the last rails all the way into the wooden ties and left others half-driven to be finished by the visiting dignitaries. Then the superintendents of the two railroads, James Strobridge of the Central Pacific and Samuel Reed of the Union Pacific, slid the laurel tie carefully under the junction where the Central Pacific rails met the rails of the Union Pacific.

The ceremony began a few minutes before 12:30 local time with a prayer by a Massachusetts minister who was there as a reporter for two religious newspapers. In response to a flurry of messages from telegraph offices in the the East, the Union Pacific operator at Promontory tapped out a message that traveled by wire around the country: "Almost ready. Hats off. Prayer is being offered." A friend of Leland Stanford who accompanied him to the ceremony remembered a wonderful feeling of being connected to the whole nation during the prayer. "As we uncovered our heads," he later wrote, "the crowds that were gathered at the various telegraph offices in the land uncovered theirs. It was a sublime moment, and we realized it."

When the prayer was over, various dignitaries drove in some of the last iron spikes on the final pair of rails. At 12:40, after receiving yet another question from an impatient Eastern operator, the Union Pacific man tapped out: "We have got done praying. The spike is about to be presented."

There were four special spikes, two of gold—both from California— one of silver from Nevada, and another of silver, gold, and iron from Arizona. The official last golden spike had the words "The Last Spike" engraved on the top and other messages on the sides, including one that read: "The Pacific Railroad; Ground Broken January 8, 1863; completed May 8, 1869." It was now May 10, but the engraver could never have predicted the strange turn of events.

Leland Stanford and Thomas Durant dropped the special spikes into holes drilled in the laurel tie, and Stanford accepted the spikes and other ceremonial gifts in a booming, boring speech. Then Grenville Dodge, chief engineer for the Union Pacific, spoke for Durant, whose head was still throbbing in the noonday sun. Dodge's short speech inspired the restless crowd by calling up a prediction from Missouri Senator Thomas Hart Benton, one of the greatest supporters of western expansion:

The great Benton prophecied that some day a granite statue of Columbus would be erected on the highest peak of the Rocky Mountains, pointing westward, denoting the great route across the Continent. You have made the prophecy today a fact. This is the way to India!

Cartoon from *Frank Leslie's Illustrated Newspaper,* May 29, 1869, portraying engines labeled San Francisco and New York shaking hands

Stanford had a special, silver-plated hammer, and some reporters thought the silver hammer and the official golden spike were both wired to the telegraph. But the man who did the wiring remembered a regular iron railroad hammer with a copper plate on its face and a regular iron spike with its head "carefully polished" to improve the connection. The hammer was wired to the western telegraph line and the spike to the eastern line. When the hammer came down, it would send a surge of electricity across the nation.

Durant had a regular hammer, too, and he wore long leather gloves to protect his soft hands. Standing on opposite sides of the rail, the two men probably gave the special spikes a few light, ceremonial taps. Then Stanford picked up the iron hammer, wired to the telegraph, and stood over the polished iron spike—the real last spike—which was not in the fancy laurel tie but in a regular wooden tie beside it. Durant stood ready to strike the second blow on the same spike.

Now the great moment had arrived. Stanford raised the wired hammer in the air, ready to strike the blow that would be heard from sea to shining sea. The telegraph operator tapped out three dots as a signal to cities from New York to San Francisco. Many years later, a man who was at Promontory that day claimed that when Stanford brought the hammer down he missed the spike—and Durant missed it, too. "We all yelled like to bust," the man said, and this funny story has been told and retold as if it were fact. It might be true, but none of the reports written in 1869 mentioned it.

All we know for sure is that the hammer came down, and a surge of electricity spanned the nation. In San Francisco, the electricity rang fire bells and shot off a 15-inch cannon at a fort overlooking the Pacific. Locomotive whistles blasted in Sacramento and Omaha. Mormons prayed and cheered in Salt Lake City. The people of Chicago took to the streets in "an entirely impromptu" parade that stretched for seven miles, and citizens of Buffalo sang "The Star-Spangled Banner." The bells of Independence Hall rang in Philadelphia, one hundred guns fired at New York's City Hall, and a magnetic ball fell from the Capitol dome in Washington, D.C.

Back at Promontory, Thomas Durant and Leland Stanford shook hands, and Durant proclaimed, "There is henceforth but one Pacific Railroad of the United States." The two engines met on the final rails, almost touching while the engineers climbed out and reached across the gap, breaking a champagne bottle in celebration. Some of the soldiers tapped the spikes with their swords, and a few ladies tapped them, too. Then the Central Pacific's Jupiter backed up to allow the Union Pacific's Engine 119 to cross onto the Central Pacific tracks; Engine 119 backed up to allow Jupiter to cross, demonstrating that tracks were now continuous across the country.

When the official ceremonies were over, the laurel tie and special spikes were removed for safekeeping and replaced with a regular tie and iron spikes. The crowd surged in and chipped away pieces of the wood and rails as souvenirs. The tie had to be replaced six times and the heavy rails twice before the treasure hunters were through. Whiskey flowed from the canvas tents, bands played under the warm Utah sun, and the revelers threw their hats in the desert air.

Among the soldiers who tapped the golden spike was Captain John Currier of New Hampshire. He was traveling with his new wife, Nattie, to rejoin his regiment in San Francisco. Along with other officers and their wives, John and Nattie were invited to join the dignitaries in their private cars. "Champagne flowed like water," Currier wrote in his diary. "Much nonsense was got off but we had a jolly day." Durant's special train started east around 4:30; Stanford's headed west a short while later. By six o'clock that evening, Currier noted, the crowds were gone. And then John and Nattie Currier did something no one had ever done before. They boarded a westbound train and continued their trip from the East Coast to California.

For a short while after the golden spike ceremony, Promontory was a popular stop on the transcontinental line.

THIS TRAIN

STOPS

20 Minutes for Supper at the

Golden Hotel

PROMONTORY, UTAH.

FIRST-CLASS MEALS, 50 CENTS.

THE GOLDEN SPIKE

Completing the first Trans-continental Railroad was driven at this point May 10, 1869. Don't fail to treat yourself to a first class meal at this celebrated point.

T. G. BROWN, Prop.

## Historical Note

During the 1850s the U.S. Army carried out four official surveys to locate the best route for a transcontinental railroad. By that time, the bitter conflict over slavery was heating to fever pitch, and northern politicians would not approve a railroad through the South, just as southern politicians would not approve a railroad through the North. This was the same basic conflict discussed in the previous story, between the southern Overland Mail route and the central Pony Express route. The central route along the Platte River was not even surveyed, because it was so well known, but the success of the Pony Express paved the way for the first transcontinental railroad over much of the same route.

With the outbreak of the Civil War, southern opposition took to the battlefields rather than the halls of Congress, and in 1862, President Abraham Lincoln signed the Pacific Railway Act. Serious construction began after the war, when a huge workforce of former soldiers was suddenly available. Building west from Omaha, Nebraska, the Union Pacific employed thousands of Irish immigrants, along with many other workers. The Central Pacific, building east from Sacramento, turned to Chinese laborers, some of whom were already in California for the gold rush and others who came directly from China. On the day the rails met in Promontory, the Union Pacific had completed 1,086 miles of track; the Central Pacific had completed 690 miles, including the most difficult work of all across the Sierra Nevada.

The first transcontinental railroad, along with other western railroads, changed the West forever. Towns and farms grew along the tracks where Indians had once chased buffalo. Early passengers would shoot buffalo for sport from the moving cars, leaving the carcasses to rot in the sun. The railroads also brought professional buffalo hunters, who slaughtered what was left of the great herds and sent their hides by rail back East. There were about 50 million buffalo on the Plains in the early 1840s, when western migration began along the Oregon Trail. By 1886, there were fewer than a thousand buffalo. Without this essential source of food and clothing, the once-powerful Plains Indians could no longer resist white advancement into their territory.

The western railroads also created the classic era of cowboys and cow towns. Beginning in 1866, Texas cowboys drove their herds of longhorns north to Kansas, where they shipped the animals on the Kansas Pacific, which was then building westward in competition with the Union Pacific. Other western railroads carried cattle, too, along with farm products, minerals, timber, and other goods. In 1881, the Atchison, Topeka, and Santa Fe line met the Southern Pacific in Deming, New Mexico, forming the second transcontinental railroad and ultimately creating a population boom in southern California. In 1883, a third transcontinental line was completed from Minneapolis-St. Paul to Seattle. Others followed, and the ever-growing network of iron rails across the prairies, plains, deserts, and mountains soon spelled the end of the western frontier.

*The story of the golden spike ceremony is told in many different sources, often with conflicting information— much like the story of the first ride of the Pony Express. I have used newspaper articles, eyewitness accounts, and detailed descriptions in various books that use other original sources. To sort out the conflicts, I have generally followed "Driving the Last Spike," an excellent scholarly article by J.N. Bowman, and a recent, comprehensive book* Empire Express, *by David Haward Bain.*

Lakota warriors attack Custer's troops in this drawing by Red Horse, a Lakota leader who participated in the Battle of the Little Bighorn.

## TALE № 8

# WE SHOOT, WE RIDE FAST, WE SHOOT AGAIN
### THE BATTLE OF THE LITTLE BIGHORN

1876

GEORGE ARMSTRONG CUSTER steadied his field glasses on the rugged ridge at a place called the Crow's Nest and gazed out toward the Little Bighorn River some 15 miles away. Earlier that morning, in the soft clear light of dawn, his Crow scouts had seen signs of a large Indian village in this direction. There wasn't much to see at such a distance: smoke rising from cooking fires, curly black lines like "worms crawling in the grass" that represented the pony herd. But the Crows knew this country, and they could read the signs so well that they were convinced this was a big village, perhaps the largest Indian village ever gathered on the Plains.

Now, in full morning light around 9 a.m., Custer strained to see the signs. Beside him was Mitch Boyer, one of the best scouts on the Plains. The son of a Sioux mother and a French father, Mitch had proven his loyalty to the whites, but Custer got testy when he couldn't see what Mitch and the other scouts could see.

"I've got about as good eyes as anybody," Custer muttered in disgust, "and I can't see any village, Indians, or anything else."

"Well, general," Mitch replied, "if you don't find more Indians in that valley than you ever saw together, you can hang me." Custer was only a lieutenant colonel, but Mitch and the other men always called him "general" because he had been given an honorary general's rank during the Civil War.

George Armstrong Custer

According to an officer who witnessed this conversation, Custer sprang to his feet saying, "It would do a damned sight of good to hang you, wouldn't it?" George Custer seldom swore; he was angry and wanted to see the village for himself. So he stormed down the hill and rode back to where the rest of his Seventh Cavalry waited. There he borrowed an expensive set of Austrian binoculars from Lieutenant Charles DeRudio and returned to the Crow's Nest. This time he saw some "cloud-like objects" that the scouts said were pony herds.

Custer and his men were part of a major Army effort to drive the Teton Sioux, or Lakota, and their close allies the northern Cheyenne on to the Great Sioux Reservation. Custer's original plan was to hide his men all day, so they could rest from their ride the night before, then ride again under cover of darkness to attack the village at dawn. By that time another force under Custer's commanding officer, General Alfred Terry, was supposed to be on the Bighorn River to the north, ready to capture any Indians who tried to escape. It was a reasonable plan, but Custer changed it. The scouts and some of the men had seen small parties of Lakota and Cheyenne, and they were convinced that some of these Indians had seen the main column of the Seventh Cavalry. Custer's greatest fear was that the Indians would escape and scatter on the Plains, so he decided to attack then and there in broad daylight. It was Sunday, June 25, 1876.

Around noon, Custer divided his regiment into four groups. He kept 221 men under his own command and assigned 175 men, including most of the Indian scouts, to Major Marcus Reno. Together they would follow a creek down to the Little Bighorn River. A smaller group of 115 men under Captain Frederick Benteen would ride across a series of ridges to get a better view of the Little Bighorn Valley before rejoining the main column. Another 136 men lagged behind with the slow-moving mule train that carried food and extra ammunition.

Sitting Bull

After two hours of riding along the creek, the men under Custer and Reno reached a single tepee with a dead warrior inside. It was all that remained of a large campsite. Here Custer received word from his scouts that they had seen Indians—the people who had been camped near the tepee—about 5 miles away, looking like they were running away. Custer ordered Reno to trot ahead with his troops. About 30 minutes later, he received more reports of Indians, and one of his scouts caught sight of the main village. Now Custer ordered Reno to "charge the village . . . and you will be supported by the whole outfit."

Reno's battalion forded the creek and then the Little Bighorn, approaching the great village from the south. Each band formed a camp circle; the first from this direction was a band called the Hunkpapa, led by the holy man Sitting Bull. In 1851, the whites had appointed Conquering Bear as chief of all the Lakota because he was willing to sign a treaty. Now, 25 years later, Sitting Bull—who refused to sign treaties—had emerged as the true leader of all the Lakota and Cheyenne who were willing to fight for their traditional life of following the buffalo.

A Cheyenne woman named Kate Bighead was near the Hunkpapa camp that day, visiting friends among the Lakota. "We found our women friends bathing in the river," she remembered, "and we joined them. Other groups, men, women, and children, were playing in the water at many places along the stream. Some boys were fishing. All of us were having a good time. . . . No one was thinking of any battle coming." Suddenly two boys ran toward them, shouting, "Soldiers are coming!"

We heard shooting. We hid in the brush. The sounds of the shooting multiplied—pop—pop—pop—pop! We heard women and children screaming. Old men were calling the young warriors to battle. Young men were singing their war songs as they responded to the call. Throngs of Sioux men on horses were racing toward the skirt of timber just south of the Uncpapa [Hunkpapa] camp circle, where the guns were clattering. The horsemen warriors were dodging through a mass of women, children, and old people hurrying afoot to the benchland hills west of the camps.

Although they had been caught by surprise, the Indians quickly organized their forces. "The very earth seemed to grow Indians," Reno later wrote. He formed a skirmish line at the edge of the camp, with every fourth man leading the horses into the protection of cottonwood trees along the river. The Indians easily rode around the line, shooting at them from front and back. Reno ordered a retreat, but steady rifle fire forced them into the trees and then across the river, picking them off "at will" according to one survivor. Finally the soldiers climbed a network of ravines and gathered on the high bluffs above the river. In less than an hour, 40 men under Reno's command had been killed and 13 wounded. Another 17 were left behind in the trees.

Soon after Reno's men reached the bluffs, Captain Benteen arrived, carrying a note from one of Custer's officers: "Benteen. Come on. Big Village. Be quick. Bring packs. P. [S.] Bring pacs." Benteen understood that packs meant extra ammunition, and this was the second such order he had received. Yet neither he nor Major Reno responded to the order. Reno was concerned with his dead and wounded, and he ordered Benteen to form a skirmish line to protect his men from the Indians who were still attacking from below. Five minutes later, they heard the sound of heavy firing to the north. Then, strangely, mysteriously, the attacking Indians headed up the river. It was 4:30 p.m.

●  ●  ●

AN HOUR AND A HALF EARLIER, after sending Reno to attack the village, Custer had led his men along the opposite bank of the Little Bighorn and up the high bluffs where Reno and Benteen were now positioned. It was from the bluffs that Custer finally saw the village, spread below him like a sea of white three miles long on the other side of the Little Bighorn River. According to Sergeant Daniel Kanipe, "The boys began to cheer. Some of the horses became so excited that some riders were unable to hold them in ranks."

"Hold your horses in, boys," Custer shouted. "There are plenty of them down there for all of us."

He was right. There were about 1,000 lodges with perhaps 7,000 people: about 2,000 fighting men and older boys and 5,000 women, children, and elders. Custer had a little less than 600 officers and soldiers, with another 50 scouts and civilians, divided into four different groups. Two of those groups were nowhere to be found; Reno and his men were pinned down by heavy enemy fire.

Custer sent Sergeant Kanipe back to find Captain Benteen and the pack train. Then he led his men farther north, where he climbed another high point and again surveyed the scene with binoculars. In the valley below, Lieutenant DeRudio—who had lent Custer the binoculars that morning—could clearly see his commander high on the hill, waving his hat against the big Montana sky. That was the last time any of the other men in the Seventh Cavalry saw Custer or his command alive.

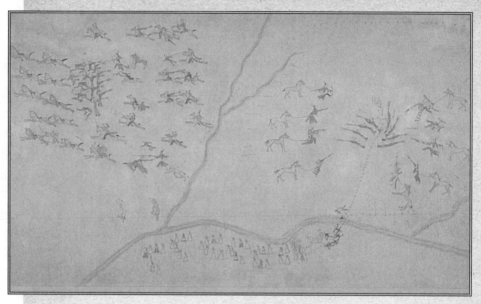

Custer's last stand (above, left) and Reno's retreat and later fighting (above, right) are portrayed simultaneously in this map by a Cheyenne warrior named White Bird.

Historians differ on where Custer was standing and exactly what he could see, but whatever he saw, he decided he really needed Benteen and that extra ammunition. So he ordered trumpeter John Martin to carry another message. Martin, whose real name was Giovani Martini, was from Italy. His English was not too good, so an officer quickly scribbled the note that Benteen later showed to Reno when they met on the hill.

Custer now led his men into a large, dry gulch called Medicine Tail Coulee, which ran down to the Little Bighorn. About this time, his younger brother Boston arrived from the rear with news that he had passed Benteen a few miles back. Another brother, Tom, was already with George, as were his nephew and brother-in-law. The Custers were a close family who believed in sharing the glory—and the danger. Boston's news seemed encouraging, because Custer assumed that Benteen would obey his order to hurry and bring the extra ammunition. Then Mitch Boyer, who had been watching the valley below, brought some bad news: Reno's

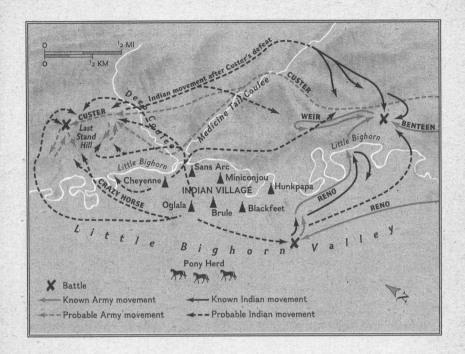

Little Bighorn Valley

- ✕ Battle
- ←— Known Army movement
- ←- - Probable Army movement
- ←— Known Indian movement
- ←- - Probable Indian movement

battalion had been defeated; they were fleeing desperately across the river.

Hoping to draw the Indians away from Reno, Custer divided his command—now about 210 men—into two wings, one under Captain George Yates, the other under Captain Myles Keogh. Keogh's troops stayed on the high bluffs, while Yates and his men thundered down Medicine Tail Coulee toward the river, bugles blaring, horses kicking dust in the air. Custer hoped that this loud display would not only turn attention away from Reno but also frighten the Indians and make them believe there were more soldiers than there really were. The men drew light fire from the village before turning back to head up the bluffs and join Keogh's men. Just as Custer intended, this fake attack shifted the battle away from Reno, allowing the survivors of Reno's battalion to defend themselves on the bluffs.

Custer and the Yates wing rode still farther north, perhaps to look for another place to cross the river and capture the women, children, and elders who were now fleeing in terror. By capturing the warriors' families, he might force the warriors to surrender. Some historians have thought that he met a large attacking force led by the great Lakota warrior Crazy Horse, who drove the soldiers back to the high ground. Recent research, however, suggests that Crazy Horse took a different route, and Custer may have turned back because he still thought everything was under control—that Benteen and the ammunition would arrive, perhaps even that Reno would regroup and join them. If that were true, there would be time to capture the fleeing Indians after the soldiers defeated the warriors. But it wasn't true.

The Indians who had been fighting Reno on the south end of the village moved quickly toward the north to answer the new threat from the charging bluecoats. They crossed the river near Medicine Tail Coulee and moved cautiously up the hills where Keogh's men held the high ground. "The shooting at first was at a distance," recalled a Cheyenne warrior, "but we kept creeping in closer all around the ridge." Two large forces, one led by a Cheyenne chief named Lame White Man, the other led by a Hunkpapa chief named Gall, pounded the soldiers with bullets and iron-tipped arrows. Then Crazy Horse and White Bull, a nephew of Sitting Bull, made a mad dash through the bluecoats, drawing a barrage of fire but emerging untouched.

Crazy Horse's charge split Keogh's troops in two. Those to the rear died in small groups, while the survivors joined Custer and Yates's men on a small rounded hill to the north—a little more than 100 soldiers surrounded by some 1,500 Indian warriors. A Cheyenne named Two Moons described the scene:

> Then the shooting was quick, quick. Pop—pop—pop very fast. Some of the soldiers were down on their knees, some standing. Officers all in front. The smoke was like a great cloud, and everywhere the Sioux went the dust rose like smoke. We circled all around them—swirling like water round a stone. We

Crazy Horse rides through the battle in this drawing by Amos Bad Heart Bull, who was a child with Crazy Horse's band at the Little Bighorn.

shoot, we ride fast, we shoot again. Soldiers drop, and horses fall on them. Soldiers in line drop, but one man rides up and down the line—all the time shouting. He rode a sorrel horse with white face and white fore-legs. I don't know who he was. He was a brave man.

The brave man may have been Custer, who rode a horse that matched Two Moons's description. Many fought bravely that afternoon, but others panicked. Some were unable to fire their guns; some fired wildly into the air; a few committed suicide. The last to die were not on the hill at all but in a deep ravine, where they dashed in a desperate attempt to escape.

Custer's body was found near the top of the hill, a bullet hole in his left temple and another near his heart, stripped naked but otherwise unmutilated—a sign of respect for a brave warrior. Or at least he appeared unmutilated to the eyes of those who found him. Kate Bighead remembered that two Cheyenne women who recognized Custer from his

"The Last Glow of a Passing Nation," by Richard Lorenz (1914) evokes the mixed emotions of victory and defeat for the Indian people.

fighting against their people in the south "pushed the point of a sewing awl into each of his ears . . . to improve his hearing, as it seemed he had not heard what our chiefs in the South said when he smoked the pipe with them." Many of the other bodies were mutilated beyond recognition.

As they listened to the firing in the distance, some of the officers under Reno and Benteen wanted to join Custer, but Reno refused to give the order. Just after 5 p.m., without any orders at all, Captain Thomas B. Weir—one of Benteen's officers—led his company toward the firing. Three other companies followed, including that of Captain Benteen. Reno, with the rest of the command and the wounded, brought up the rear, but all of them were too late. When the first riders reached a high point where they could see the battle in the distance, they realized that the battle was over. "We saw a good many Indians galloping up and down and firing at objects on the ground," one officer recalled. ". . . I know the men must have all been killed from the scattering fire and firing down at the ground."

Soon "a good many" Indians turned in their direction and drove them back to their original position on what is now called Reno Hill. There the soldiers formed a circular skirmish line in a natural depression, with their wounded in the middle, as Indian snipers—now armed with carbines they had taken from Custer's men—peppered away from every hill and ridge in the rolling, grassy landscape. "They pounded at us all of what was left of the first day," said Benteen, and it wasn't until darkness fell around 9 p.m. that the shooting stopped. That night, as they listened to dancing and singing in the village below, the troopers dug shallow trenches and piled whatever they could find—packs, saddles, ammunition boxes, and dead horses and mules—in front of them for protection.

At dawn the trumpeters sounded reveille, and almost on cue the fighting began again with a shower of arrows and bullets from every side. Captain Benteen, who had been so slow to answer Custer's order, now proved himself an inspiring leader, standing in full view of the Indians as he barked orders and led a daring assault. Benteen even persuaded the timid Major Reno to lead an attack when the Indians came too close. But there were too many Indians and too few soldiers. As the day grew hotter, the men suffered desperately from thirst—especially the wounded—and a brave party of volunteers rushed down to the river for water. Then, in the early afternoon, the shooting began to die down, growing less and less. That evening the Indians set fire to the grass along the river to create a smoke screen, and the entire village moved on.

The Battle of the Little Bighorn was over, and though the Indians didn't know it as they moved up the river, so was the old, free life of the Lakota and the Cheyenne.

## Historical Note

In 1868, the U.S. government signed a new treaty with the Sioux and northern Cheyenne at Fort Laramie. This treaty established the Great Sioux Reservation in what is now western South Dakota and allowed the Indians to hunt buffalo in what is now Montana. Although some leaders signed the treaty and moved their people to the reservation, others, including Sitting Bull and Crazy Horse, did not sign and refused to give up their traditional way of life.

The situation grew tense in 1874 when George Armstrong Custer led an expedition into the Black Hills and reported "gold among the roots of the grass." The Black Hills were part of the Great Sioux Reservation, but white people wanted the gold. The government offered to buy the hills and the hunting grounds. Some Indian leaders were willing to sell if the price was high enough, but Sitting Bull and Crazy Horse would not even attend the conference. When the two sides were unable to reach an agreement, President Ulysses S. Grant ordered all Sioux and

northern Cheyenne to report to government agencies by January 31, 1876, or face military action.

That spring the Army attacked the Montana hunting grounds from the west, south, and east. Custer's Seventh Cavalry was part of the eastern thrust out of Fort Abraham Lincoln in what is now North Dakota. On June 17, the southern thrust under General George Crook was surprised by warriors under Crazy Horse and Sitting Bull in the Rosebud Valley, just across the divide from the Little Bighorn Valley. Although Crook declared a "victory," the battle was fairly even and the general retreated.

A week later, Custer passed through the Rosebud Valley and followed the Indian trail to the Little Bighorn. He had no way of knowing what Crook had learned about their fighting abilities, and he did not know that the village had more than doubled in size that week, swelled by new arrivals from the reservation who had come to join their relatives for the summer hunt. Custer stumbled on the largest number of warriors ever gathered together on the Plains, and they were more organized and willing to fight than ever before.

Ironically, the greatest Indian victory led to their final defeat. News of the "Custer Massacre" enflamed public opinion; by the end of July, Congress had approved funds to build two new forts along the Yellowstone River, added 2,500 cavalry troops, and given the Army control over the Sioux agencies. That August, all rations for the Sioux were cut off until they gave up their claims to the Black Hills and the Montana hunting grounds. It was "sign or starve," so the chiefs on the reservation signed the treaty. In the meantime, the great village of Sitting Bull had broken into smaller groups to find grass for their horses and food for themselves. General Crook destroyed one village and occupied the Black Hills, but even more devastating was a relentless winter campaign led by Colonel Nelson Miles. In early May, Sitting Bull and about a thousand followers crossed into Canada. On May 6, 1877, Crazy Horse surrendered. The Great Sioux War was over.

*In telling this story, I have used eyewitness accounts from soldiers and scouts and from Lakota and Cheyenne who fought the soldiers or observed the battle. Other information has come from archaeological evidence gathered from the battlefield after a wildfire in 1983.*

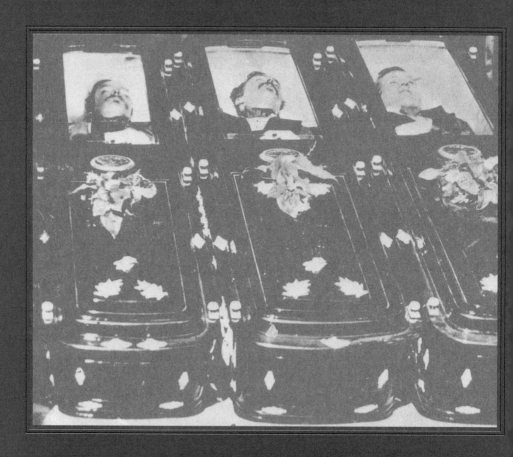

The victims of the Tombstone showdown in their expensive,
silver-trimmed caskets: (left to right) Tom McLaury, Frank McLaury,
and Billy Clanton

THROUGHOUT THE WEST, BOOMTOWNS SPRANG UP LIKE MAGIC WHEREVER GOLD OR SILVER WAS FOUND. MEN FOUGHT TO CONTROL THESE TOWNS WITH LAWS, MONEY, AND GUNS. SOMETIMES IT WAS HARD TO TELL THE GOOD GUYS FROM THE BAD GUYS.

## TALE № 9

# THROW UP YOUR HANDS!

### SHOWDOWN IN TOMBSTONE

IT WAS AFTER MIDNIGHT when Ike Clanton stumbled into the lunchroom of the Alhambra Saloon for a late-night meal. Ike lived on a ranch outside of town, and he had come into Tombstone a few hours earlier with his friend Tom McLaury to take care of business and do some drinking and gambling. By the time he decided to eat, Ike had had plenty to drink. In the lunchroom, he ran into another man who drank too much—a gunslinging gambler named John H. Holliday, nicknamed Doc because he had once been trained as a dentist.

Doc swore at Ike and told him to get a gun and fight. Ike replied that he didn't have a gun. Only law officers were allowed to carry a gun in Tombstone, so Ike had left his guns at the Grand Hotel across the street. Doc probably didn't have a gun, either, but he was full of whiskey and fury. The two men argued and cursed each other in the lunchroom at the front of the Alhambra Saloon.

Bad blood between them had been boiling for months, ever since Doc had been arrested for a stagecoach robbery and two murders committed by some of Ike's friends. Although Doc was released, he was still angry. As for Ike—he was scared. He had made a deal with Doc's friend Wyatt

Earp to betray his own friends for the stagecoach reward money, and now he was afraid that Doc or Wyatt or both would "spill the beans" and get him killed as a traitor.

Wyatt Earp sat at the counter in the lunchroom that night, and as the argument between Doc and Ike got louder, he motioned to his younger brother Morgan, who was standing at the bar of the saloon just beyond the counter. Morgan was a police officer, so he carried a gun. He jumped over the counter and moved the argument out into the street, but Morgan was just as hot-headed as Doc and Ike. He only made the situation worse, threatening and cursing at Ike while Ike cursed and threatened back.

Just then Virgil Earp appeared from the Occidental Saloon next door. Almost five years older than Wyatt and eight years older than Morgan, Virgil was the chief of police in Tombstone, a position sometimes called the town marshal. He calmly and clearly told Ike and Doc that he would throw them in jail if they didn't stop arguing. Wyatt tried to calm them down, too. Virgil and Wyatt were different from Ike or Doc or Morgan. On a wild frontier where men drank day and night, Virgil and Wyatt seldom drank at all. They knew that being sober gave them an edge when it came to a fight. Even better, being sober helped them avoid fights. And that's what they tried to do in the early morning of October 26, 1881.

John H. "Doc" Holliday

The group broke up after Virgil's warning. Ike crossed the street to the Grand Hotel, where he was staying for the night, and came back outside with his Colt revolver. He ran into Wyatt and asked him to walk with him through the dark streets. "This fighting talk has been going on for a long time," Ike said, "and I guess it's about time to fetch it to a close."

"I'll fight no one if I can get away from it," Wyatt replied, "because there's no money in it." It was an odd answer that reflected Wyatt's true interests as a gambler and a businessman rather than a gunfighter.

"I will be ready for you in the morning," Ike replied, as he walked away and disappeared into the darkness.

That's the way Wyatt later told the story. It's unlikely that Ike really threatened to fight Wyatt or the Earp brothers along with Doc; but it's true that long before the stage robbery, bad feelings had begun to fester between the Earps and Ike's family and friends, a group of men known in Tombstone as "the cowboys." Some folks in Tombstone liked the Earps and hated the cowboys. Some folks hated the Earps and liked the cowboys. It was a confusing situation.

After closing up a gambling game he was running, Wyatt met Doc Holliday on the street and walked him to his rooming house, which was owned by photographer Camillus Fly. Then Wyatt went home. Ike, too keyed up to sleep, headed for the Occidental Saloon with his pistol in his belt and got into a poker game. Sitting around the table that night were Ike and his friend Tom McLaury along with a few other men and the two most powerful law officers in Tombstone: Virgil Earp and Johnny Behan. Johnny was the county sheriff and a good friend of the cowboys. Johnny and Virgil often argued about what to do and who was in charge; yet here they were, playing cards all night with Ike

Joseph Isaac "Ike" Clanton

Clanton and Tom McLaury. Ike later recalled that Virgil kept his pistol on his lap. Virgil must have seen Ike's pistol, but he probably figured it was better to keep an eye on him than to challenge him then and there.

The poker game broke up at dawn, and Virgil went home to catch a few hours' sleep. When his wife, Allie, asked him what he'd been doing all night, he said, "Oh, I been tryin' to keep Ike Clanton and Doc Holliday from killin' each other."

"Why didn't you let 'em go ahead?" Allie asked. "Neither one amounts to much."

Ike Clanton never went to sleep at all. At eight in the morning, a bartender on his way home from work met him in the street with his pistol in full view. "As soon as the Earps and Doc Holliday show themselves in the street," Ike claimed, "the ball will open and they will have to fight." The bartender went to warn Wyatt Earp, but Wyatt just stayed in bed. One of Virgil's deputies tried to rouse him with a similar warning, but Virgil stayed in bed, too.

All that morning Ike wandered around town, drinking and making threats. He obtained a Winchester rifle to go with his Colt revolver and went over to Camillus Fly's rooming house to look for Doc Holliday. Doc was still sleeping, but his girlfriend, Big Nose Kate, was looking through some photographs when Ike entered Fly's studio, carrying the Winchester. She woke Doc to warn him that Ike was looking for him. "If God will let me live long enough," Doc replied, "he will see me."

It was shortly after noon when Virgil and Wyatt finally appeared in the streets, joined by Morgan and their oldest brother, James. They had received more reports of threats from Ike, and they knew he was carrying a rifle along with the six-shooter. James had been wounded in the Civil War, so he wasn't much for fighting, but the others went looking for Ike. Virgil and Morgan found him coming out of a saloon on Fourth Street. Virgil sneaked up from behind, grabbing the Winchester with his left hand while smashing Ike across the head with a pistol. Ike went sprawling on the wooden sidewalk with blood flowing from his skull.

Wyatt arrived moments later and the Earp brothers marched Ike Clanton to a nearby courtroom. While Virgil went to get the judge, Morgan and Wyatt watched Ike. For the first time since the trouble began, Wyatt Earp lost his cool. According to the county clerk, Wyatt swore at Ike and called him a cattle thief. "You've threatened my life enough," he growled, "and you've got to fight." Just the night before, Wyatt had said he'd try to avoid a fight. Maybe now he was tired and grumpy; maybe he'd just had enough of Ike.

**Virgil Earp**     **Wyatt Earp**     **Morgan Earp**

"Fight is my racket," Ike shot back, "and all I want is four feet of ground." Ike said he'd shoot it out then and there if he had a gun. One of the Earp brothers offered Ike a gun, but the deputy sheriff stopped him. The judge fined Ike $25 plus $2.50 in court costs for carrying a weapon in town. That was a lot of money in those days, but Ike paid it in cash.

As Wyatt left the courtroom, he ran into Tom McLaury. Wyatt later claimed that Tom threatened him, too, but most folks around Tombstone thought Tom was the least likely of all the cowboys to look for a fight. It's possible that Tom was carrying a gun that day, but no one saw it. What they did see was Wyatt slapping Tom across the face with his left hand while he raised his six-shooter with his right hand and smashed Tom across the head, just like Virgil had done to Ike. Now things were getting downright ugly.

Around this time, Ike's younger brother, Billy, and Tom's older brother, Frank, rode into town. Billy Clanton was only 19 years old, but he was already a good shot. Frank McLaury was in his 30s and considered the best man with a gun in the county. They were coming into town to meet their brothers and take care of business. But they soon discovered what had been going on, and the nature of their business quickly changed.

The Clantons and McLaurys gathered in a gun shop, where Wyatt and Virgil could clearly see them buying ammunition. Ike tried to buy a gun, but he was in such bad shape from the head wound and continuous drinking that the store owner refused to sell it to him. Later the Clantons and McLaurys visited a stable on Allen Street and then crossed through the O.K. Corral to Fremont Street. Maybe they were going to leave town peacefully; maybe they weren't.

Virgil ran into Johnny Behan outside Hafford's Saloon, and the two lawmen stepped inside to discuss the situation. According to Johnny, he asked Virgil to disarm the cowboys and Virgil refused, saying he was ready for a fight. Virgil told a different story, saying he asked Johnny to help him disarm the cowboys and Johnny refused. When they left the saloon, several concerned townspeople approached them, including a representative of the Citizens Safety Group who offered Virgil "25 armed men at a minute's notice." The prospect of a citizen's army taking the law into their own hands spurred Johnny Behan to take action. He decided to go and disarm the cowboys himself.

He found Frank McLaury holding his horse on Fremont Street, but Frank refused to give up his gun unless the Earps gave up theirs. Johnny and Frank then walked down Fremont to a vacant lot next to Camillus Fly's rooming house, where Tom McLaury and the Clanton brothers had gathered with a friend named Billy Claiborne. Ike later claimed they were on their way to get his wagon and leave town, but they didn't have to pass through the lot to do that, and the lot happened to be right next to Doc Holliday's room. Johnny searched Ike and Tom and decided they weren't armed, but Frank McLaury and Billy Clanton still refused to give up their guns. As Johnny walked away, a bystander heard one of the cowboys say, "You need not be afraid, Johnny, we are not going to have any trouble."

By now, the Earp brothers and Doc Holliday had decided to disarm the cowboys themselves, walking down Fourth Street and turning up Fremont. It was a cold, windy afternoon in the high desert, and Doc, who was sick with tuberculosis, wore a long, gray overcoat. Virgil and Morgan wore shorter, black coats, and Wyatt may have had two coats: a short one like his brothers and a longer overcoat with special leather pockets for his revolvers. Virgil walked in the lead, carrying Doc's silver-headed cane in his left hand. Wyatt, Doc, and Morgan trailed behind, Doc holding Virgil's shotgun beneath his overcoat.

Johnny Behan approached the Earps on Fremont Street near the rear entrance of the O.K. Corral. He told them to go back and that he was there to disarm the cowboys. The Earps thought he meant that he had actually

The Earp Brothers and Doc Holliday begin their now-famous walk down Fourth Street.

taken their guns, so Virgil switched Doc's cane to his shooting hand and put his six-shooter in the left side of his pants. Wyatt put his revolver in the pocket of his overcoat. Then they brushed past Johnny Behan as if he weren't even there. Johnny followed a few steps behind.

If Virgil and Wyatt were hoping for a peaceful outcome, Morgan and Doc had other plans. As they passed a butcher shop, a woman buying meat heard Morgan say, "Let them have it!" and Doc reply, "All right." She could clearly see the shotgun as Doc's coat flapped open in the wind.

The Earps and Holliday faced off with the cowboys in the lot next to Fly's rooming house—just 15 feet wide, not much room for 9 men and 2 horses. "Boys, throw up your hands!" Virgil shouted. "I want your guns!"

Tom McLaury opened his vest to show he wasn't armed. The Earps later claimed that Frank McLaury and Billy Clanton cocked their six-shooters, and Virgil cried, "Hold on, I don't want that!" Other witnesses claimed that it was Morgan and Doc who raised their guns first and that Virgil was talking to them.

Suddenly two shots rang out, so close together that they had to be fired by two different guns. Virgil and Wyatt said that Billy Clanton shot first, missing his aim, and Wyatt shot next, hitting Frank McLaury squarely in the stomach. Ike Clanton and Billy Claiborne said the first two shots came from Doc and Morgan. A more objective witness also "had the impression" that the "Earp party" fired first.

After a moment's pause a barrage of shots echoed across the vacant lot. Billy Claiborne ran for cover behind Fly's rooming house. Johnny Behan ran through the house and met him in the back. Ike Clanton—who'd been looking for a fight all day—ran away, too, through the rooming house into another vacant lot, finally ending up two blocks away. Tom McLaury tried to reach a rifle slung on Billy Clanton's horse. Doc Holliday blasted him with the shotgun, sending him stumbling out of the lot and into the street. Morgan Earp shot Billy Clanton in the chest from just a few feet away. Frank and Billy were both down with serious wounds, but they kept firing. Morgan took a bullet in the shoulder, and Virgil was hit in the calf.

Frank tried to move out into the street behind his horse, but the horse ran away, leaving him exposed. As Doc went after him with his nickel-plated pistol, Frank took aim with his revolver and said, "I've got you now."

"Blaze away," Doc replied. Frank fired; the bullet passed through Doc's pocket, grazing his hip. "I am shot right through!" he yelled. Frank staggered to the wooden sidewalk, where Doc and Morgan finished him off while Wyatt and Virgil fired at Billy. Then the gunshots ended, leaving a haze of sulfur-smelling smoke. The fight lasted less than 30 seconds.

Only Wyatt escaped untouched. According to an eyewitness, he "stood up and fired in rapid succession, as cool as a cucumber."

Frank McLaury died on the sidewalk. His brother, Tom, and Billy Clanton were carried into a nearby house, where Tom died without saying a word. Billy lasted longer, moaning in pain until a doctor injected him with morphine. "Good-bye, boys," he finally said. "Go away and let me die."

One researcher's version of the moment Virgil Earp (with cane) is wounded; (l-r) Frank McLaury, Doc Holliday, Morgan Earp (on the ground), Virgil, Wyatt Earp, Tom McLaury, and Billy Clanton

The next day, the *Tombstone Epitaph* expressed one view of the shoot-out: "The feeling among the best class of our citizens is that the Marshall was entirely justified in his efforts to disarm these men, and that being fired upon they had to defend themselves, which they did most bravely."

Another point of view was expressed by a large sign in the window of the funeral parlor where the dead cowboys were displayed: MURDERED IN THE STREETS OF TOMBSTONE.

Which was it? Who was right? Who was wrong? Or was there only in between? The argument over this 30-second gunfight has raged for 120 years, but the truth blew away on the desert wind.

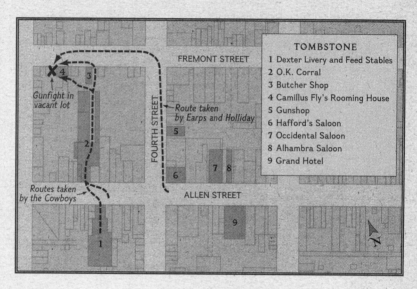

TOMBSTONE
1 Dexter Livery and Feed Stables
2 O.K. Corral
3 Butcher Shop
4 Camillus Fly's Rooming House
5 Gunshop
6 Hafford's Saloon
7 Occidental Saloon
8 Alhambra Saloon
9 Grand Hotel

FREMONT STREET

Gunfight in vacant lot

FOURTH STREET

Route taken by Earps and Holliday

Routes taken by the Cowboys

ALLEN STREET

## Historical Note

Tombstone was a typical western boomtown that sprang up in a rich silver-mining area of southeastern Arizona Territory, near the Mexican border. The colorful name came from prospector Ed Shieffelin, who first found silver in 1877. Soldiers at a nearby camp told him that he'd find his tombstone if he kept prospecting while the Apaches remained hostile to whites. Like all boomtowns, Tombstone attracted "men of restless blood," as Wyatt Earp described himself. Wyatt and his two older brothers, James and Virgil, arrived with their wives in late 1879, just as the town was starting to boom. Morgan and his wife joined them later, as did Doc Holliday and his girlfriend, Big Nose Kate. The fifth and youngest Earp brother, Warren, also came to Tombstone, but he was not involved in the shoot-out.

The Earps were a big family who stuck together, and the fact that Virgil, Wyatt, and Morgan all worked as law officers at various times soon put them in conflict with a loosely organized group of men known as the cowboys. Some of the cowboys were hardened outlaws; others—like the Clanton family—were cattle rustlers who specialized in stealing livestock from Mexico. Still others—like Frank and Tom McLaury—were real ranchers who occasionally engaged in dishonest business. The cowboys were southerners and Democrats; the Earps were northerners and Republicans, a basic conflict in many western towns. Adding to the situation was the fact that Johnny Behan and Wyatt Earp both wanted the same job as county sheriff, and both fell in love with the same woman, a beautiful young actress named Josephine Marcus. Johnny got the job, but Wyatt got Josephine.

There were several incidents that created the feud between the Earps and the cowboys, but it was the stagecoach robbery, with the arrest of Doc Holliday and the deal between Ike Clanton and Wyatt Earp, that led directly to the shoot-out. After the shoot-out, Ike Clanton filed murder charges against the Earps and Doc Holliday. A month-long legal inquiry brought forth many witnesses with conflicting evidence. This inquiry was a hearing to decide if the evidence was sufficient to put the four men on trial. Judge Wells Spicer, who presided over the hearing, criticized Virgil Earp's judgment but ruled that the Earps and Holliday were acting as law officers and the killings were "a necessary act done in the discharge of an official duty." A month later Virgil Earp was ambushed while crossing the street, leaving his left arm shattered and useless for the rest of his life. Then, in March 1882, Morgan Earp was killed while playing pool. Evidence pointed to the cowboys, and Wyatt Earp, along with Doc Holliday and Warren Earp, went after them with a vengeance, killing at least three men before riding out of Arizona Territory. Although Wyatt claimed that he had legal authority to go after the cowboys, his authority was questionable at best.

*This story is based primarily on witness testimony at the coroner's inquest, held on October 28–29, 1881, and the Spicer hearing, held from October 31 to November 28. All of this testimony has been collected and edited by Alford E. Turner in* The O.K. Corral Inquest. *I have used articles published in October 1881 Tombstone newspapers.*

SCALES AND SUMMIT OF CHILKOOT PASS    COPYRIGHT 1898. E.A.Hegg.

A long line of stampeders climb the "golden stairs" of the Chilkoot Pass on their way to the Klondike goldfields in this photo by E.A. Hegg, taken in early 1898.

EVER SINCE THE CALIFORNIA GOLD RUSH, ADVENTUROUS MEN AND WOMEN HAD SEARCHED FOR THE NEXT BIG FIND. DESPITE BIG AND SMALL DISCOVERIES, SOME KEPT SEEKING FOR THE SAKE OF THE SEARCH . . . UNTIL THEY REACHED THE LAST FRONTIER.

## TALE №10

# GOLD! GOLD! GOLD!

### THE KLONDIKE STAMPEDE

**1896**

SKOOKUM JIM WAS ON HIS WAY to visit his mother, who lived at a village now called Carcross, for "Caribou Crossing," in Canada's Yukon Territory. Jim lived in Tagish, about 20 miles away, and after walking all day in the cold north wind, he stopped to rest near a small, clear mountain lake. Leaning back against a tree, Jim fell asleep and dreamed of a beautiful lady, "pure—just like you can see through her, just like shining, gold shining." The lady wanted to marry him, but Jim already had a wife.

"Well," the lady said, "if you can't go with me, I'll give you my walking stick." She explained that he had saved her once when she was near starvation, and she had healed him when he was injured. "You're going to find the bottom of this walking stick," she told him. "You're going to find it this way." Jim looked at the bottom of the stick and saw that it was shining like gold. Finally the lady pointed north, toward the Yukon River. "You go down this way and you're going to have your luck."

Jim woke up, covered with a foot of snow. When he reached his mother's house, he discovered that he'd slept for a whole day beneath that tree—or maybe it was seven days. It depends who's telling the story. Jim believed that the beautiful lady was Wealth Woman, a spirit of good

**111**

fortune, and that he had met her once before, when he saved a frog that was stuck in a ditch far from water. Jim's people, the Tagish Indians, considered the frog to be a powerful spirit-helper.

Jim forgot about his dream for a while, but sometime later, in the summer of 1896, he decided to head north down the Yukon River in search of his sister, Kate, and her husband, George Carmack. George was a white man from California, and he had been in the Far North for more than a decade, prospecting for gold, hunting, fishing, trapping, and trading. George and Jim had once been the best of friends, but they had split apart in 1889 when Jim and his nephew, Charlie, refused to go prospecting in an area they considered full of bad spirits.

Skookum Jim with his wife, Mary, and his daughter, Daisy

George Carmack with his wife, Kate, and his daughter, Graphie Gracie

George was different from most white men. He admired the Indian people and tried to live off the land like the Indians. He spoke at least two Indian dialects. Other white prospectors thought George was too close to the "Siwashes," a negative name they used for the Indians of the upper Yukon. They called him a Squaw Man or Siwash George. Instead of being offended, George took this as a compliment.

In the spring of 1896, George, Kate, and their three-year-old daughter, Graphie Gracie, visited Forty Mile, a mining town on the Yukon River. There, George had "a very vivid dream" of two large salmon shooting up the rapids of a small stream. They stopped in front of the bank where he was sitting. "They were two beautiful fish," he later wrote, "but I noticed that instead of having scales like salmon, they were covered with an armour of bright gold nuggets and gold pieces for eyes."

George thought hard about this dream and decided it meant that he should go fishing—a strange interpretation considering the fish were covered with gold and all around him men were desperately searching for the precious metal. On July 18, 1896, George and his family left Forty Mile and headed up the Yukon about 50 miles to the mouth of a smaller stream called the Klondike. They camped on the shore with some local Indian people and began to catch and dry salmon. That's where Jim found them. He had traveled more than 500 miles downriver with Charlie and Charlie's 17-year-old brother, Patsy. It was hard to row upriver against the current, so they decided to stay and fish with George and Kate until winter. When the river froze, they would be able to walk back home.

Sometime in early August, a white prospector named Robert Henderson visited their camp and told George about gold he had found on a creek that flowed into the Klondike. Henderson was a highly respected prospector, but he was a racist. Although he encouraged George to come over and stake a claim, he made it clear that George's relatives were not welcome because he didn't want any "damned Siwashes" on his creek.

After Henderson left, Jim expressed his disgust to George. How could Henderson search for gold on Indian land, he wondered, and hunt Indian moose and caribou, but not want Indians staking claims on his creek? George told Jim not to worry about it—they would find a creek of their own. But first they decided to check out Henderson's find.

Leaving Patsy at the campsite with Kate and Graphie, the three men poled their boat two miles up the Klondike to a small tributary called Rabbit Creek. Jim had recently scouted this creek for timber, because George had a plan to cut logs and float them down to the sawmill at Forty Mile. Panning for gold along the way, Jim had found a little "color" in the sand and gravel. That didn't mean much; you could find color almost anywhere in the Yukon. But now, as they walked through wet moss, black muck, and thorny brush, they found enough traces of gold to suggest the creek might be worth a serious look if Henderson's find didn't work out.

Finally, the men climbed over a ridge and reached Henderson's camp on what he called Gold Bottom Creek. Jim and Charlie tried to buy some tobacco from Henderson, but he refused, offending them once again. George and his relatives prospected on the creek and staked claims, but they weren't impressed. So the three men recrossed the ridge to Rabbit Creek. Henderson later claimed that George promised to tell him if he found anything interesting. George claimed he asked Henderson to join them on Rabbit Creek, but the veteran prospector refused because of "his childish unreasoning prejudice. . . . his obstinacy lost him a fortune."

As the three men prospected their way down Rabbit Creek, they ran out of food. Jim was the best hunter on the upper Yukon, so he hunted for meat while George and Charlie looked for gold. The hunting was difficult, and they were so weak and hungry that they could barely go on when Jim killed a moose. While he waited for the others to join him, Jim walked down to the creek for a drink of water, carrying a piece of the moose in his hand, and saw more gold than he had ever seen before.

The men were so hungry that Jim didn't tell George and Charlie about his discovery until after they had cooked and eaten the moose. George prospected a little more in the area and convinced Jim to let him stake the discovery claim, which would allow him an extra claim on the same creek. The whites would never grant an Indian such an honor, George said. Jim didn't like the idea, but he knew George was probably right, and the two friends agreed to share the profits from the extra claim.

That's Jim's story, as reported by a Canadian government surveyor who interviewed Jim, George, Charlie, and Bob Henderson shortly after the discovery. The official believed Jim, but George claimed that he made the discovery himself.

Years later, after George's death, a manuscript published under his name included many delightful, if questionable details. According to this version, George "reached down and picked up a nugget about the size of a dime . . . and bit it like a schoolboy who had found a quarter in the garbage can." He called Jim and Charlie for the pan and shovel, dug up the loose bedrock along the creek, and turned over some flat pieces, where he "could see the raw gold lying thick between the flakey slabs, like cheese sandwiches." Walking back to the rim of the creek, he set his gold pan on the ground and joined his companions in "a war-dance around that gold-pan . . . a combination war-dance . . . Scotch hornpipe, Indian foxtrot, syncopated Irish jig, and a sort of Siwash hula-hula."

Whoever made the discovery, George Carmack changed the moment he saw the gold. After years of trying to live like the Indians, he suddenly began to think again like a white man. That night, as he gazed into the dying embers of the campfire, George imagined a glorious future in the white man's world: "a trip around the world with a congenial companion, a beautiful home with well-kept lawns . . . a sum invested in government bonds—the income of which would be sufficient to enable me to enjoy the good things of life . . . and keep me comfortable for the balance of my life."

The next day, August 17, 1896, George staked the discovery claim in his own name. He also staked the extra claim he was entitled to as "discoverer" and single claims for Jim and Charlie. Then the three men rushed down the creek so fast through the thorny brush that they looked like "human pin cushions" by the time they reached the Klondike. There they met two prospectors looking for Henderson's creek, but George told them he had found something better and produced a rifle cartridge full of gold nuggets to prove it. "I felt as if I had just dealt myself a royal flush in the game of life," George recalled, "and the whole world was a jackpot."

Sending Jim back up Rabbit Creek to protect their claims, George and Charlie headed for Forty Mile to officially record them, passing the news to more prospectors along the way. On August 22, only six days after Skookum Jim shot the moose that led him to gold, 25 miners gathered at Rabbit Creek, renamed it Bonanza Creek, and carefully recorded their claims. Yet no one told Robert Henderson, working just over the ridge from the golden riches he had dreamed of all his life.

When George Carmack produced the magic rifle cartridge in a Forty Mile saloon, the rush to the Klondike was on. By the next morning, the town was empty. As the news reached men working claims in the Forty Mile area and another mining region farther north in Alaska, they all headed for the Klondike, too. The price of boats went sky-high, and that winter, when the river froze, sled dogs were even more expensive than boats.

Ironically, George didn't have enough gold to pay the $15 filing fee, so the police inspector at Forty Mile agreed to hold the claims until he could mine more. George and Charlie returned to the creek, where Jim was waiting and other men were already beginning to mine. They built a short 10-foot sluice box, a rectangular wooden trough used to wash gold out of the gravel. They had no wheelbarrow, so Jim and Charlie carried the heavy gravel to the sluice on their backs in homemade wooden boxes. Jim was incredibly strong—the name "Skookum" meant "strong" or "husky"—and Charlie worked hard, too. Using this simple system, they mined $1,400 worth of gold in three weeks, more than enough to file their claims and buy supplies for the winter.

Other men also did well on Bonanza Creek, but the richest finds were on a little tributary that became known as Eldorado Creek, where the first prospectors got six dollars' worth of gold in a single pan. Though they didn't know it at the time, the creek would prove to be the richest gold-bearing stream in the world. Almost every one of the first 40 claims

Skookum Jim on his claim in 1899

produced a half million dollars or more at a time when refined gold sold for $20 an ounce. Today, with gold selling for $290 an ounce, this would be equivalent to more than seven million dollars for each claim.

In the fall of 1896, these riches still lay below the surface. Hundreds of men scurried to stake their claims, but some walked away in disgust before they even began to dig. Most of the experienced prospectors didn't believe in the new goldfield. It was nothing but "moose pasture" they said. Some men sold what turned out be million-dollar claims for a few hundred dollars, and one claim sold for a single sack of flour. Some changed hands for nothing at all. A Seattle YMCA instructor named Thomas Lippy decided to leave his own claim and restake one that other men had abandoned—just because his wife wanted to live in a cabin, and the new claim had more timber. It also had more gold: $1,530,000 worth, the richest single claim in the Klondike.

It was not until early October that the men on Bonanza and Eldorado began to understand the value of their claims. On the third of that month, a prospector named Louis Rhodes reached bedrock below the surface. There, by the light of a candle, he stared in amazement at the glittering seams of gold that ran through the frozen clay and gravel of the old creek bed. It was what miners called the "pay streak," and this streak was so rich that Rhodes could pay other men to do the backbreaking work while he enjoyed the profits.

As the miners dug for gold on the little creeks, a town of tents and a few lonely wooden buildings rose on the swampy flats where the Klondike flowed into the Yukon, the same place where George and Kate Carmack had come to go fishing. Named Dawson City after a Canadian geologist, it grew steadily that winter, fed by a rush of men—and a few women— who were already in the Yukon or Alaska. Like other northern boomtowns, Dawson was a strange place, half-built, locked in the long, cold darkness of the arctic winter, isolated from the outside world. Food was scarce and salt literally was worth its weight in gold; laundry was so expensive that men wore their shirts until the stench forced them to throw them away. There was no writing paper and nothing to read except old newspapers, which the miners devoured with such appreciation that they threw $400 worth of gold into a contribution box.

Through the winter and early spring, there was little of anything in Dawson except gold—so much gold that on May 23, 1897, a teenage boy named Monte Snow panned $278 worth from the sawdust on the floor of a saloon. Nine days earlier, the Yukon ice had broken with an explosive roar, and a steady stream of boats began to arrive from up river. These newcomers brought welcome news of the outside world to the stir-crazy citizens of Dawson, but the real excitement came in early June, when two supply boats arrived from downriver, carrying food and whiskey. After a

Dawson City was more peaceful than most boomtowns due to the efficient Canadian authorities.

celebration with free drinks at every saloon in town, the boats headed back toward the sea carrying about 80 Klondike miners and 3 tons of gold.

At the Alaskan seaport of St. Michael, the Klondikers boarded two ocean-going steamships, one bound for Seattle, the other for San Francisco. The Seattle boat departed first, carrying most of the miners, but the San Francisco boat sailed faster, arriving on July 15, 1897. Spectators stared slackjawed as the rugged, sunburned adventurers dragged heavy suitcases full of gold down the gangplank. By the time the Seattle boat arrived two days later, the news had spread and reporters went out to meet the ship in Puget Sound. "GOLD! GOLD! GOLD! GOLD!" the headline screamed. "STACKS OF YELLOW METAL!"

The news hit America like a thunderbolt. Suddenly, hordes of men and women dropped everything and left for the Klondike, though many of them didn't even know where it was. The rush was so strange and wild that it became known as the Klondike Stampede, the last great adventure of the Wild West. And it started with the dreams and the friendship of a white man and an Indian: George Carmack and Skookum Jim.

**Historical Note**

During the second half of the 19th century, there were major mineral discoveries in Nevada, Colorado, Montana, and Arizona, as well as many lesser finds, including several in British Columbia, Canada.

In 1873, three prospectors pushed northwest from British Columbia into the vast, desolate basin of the Yukon River, which flows in a great curve north through what is now Yukon Territory, Canada, and then west across Alaska into the Bering Sea. A gold rush in Juneau, Alaska, in 1880 brought more Americans to the Far North and proved that the Alaska Purchase of 1867—called Seward's Folly by critics of Secretary of State William H. Seward—was actually one of the greatest bargains in history.

The first big find in the Yukon region came in 1886 on the Forty-mile River, named for its distance from the main trading post. There the town of Forty Mile sprang up, and though the miners were mostly Americans, they discovered that they were actually in Canada when a Canadian surveyor arrived to define the border. Other discoveries followed, including a rich find in 1894 at Birch Creek, on the Alaska side of the border just south of the Arctic Circle, where the town of Circle blossomed into the "Paris of Alaska." Most of the rich claims in the Klondike went to pioneers from these mining regions who were already in the area before the stampede began.

News of the Klondike goldfields reached America in the middle of a depression. Like the California gold rush, it created an excitement that bordered on insanity. More than 100,000 people set out for the Klondike, but less than half that number made it, because few understood the distance and difficulties before they decided to go. Although veteran prospectors recommended carrying enough supplies to last a year, many stampeders thought they could buy everything they needed along the way, and some didn't think at all. One man left with 32 pairs of moccasins, a case of pipes, a case of shoes, two Irish setters, a bulldog pup, and a lawn tennis set.

Most stampeders entered the Yukon from Alaska by crossing one of two treacherous mountain passes: the Chilkoot Pass and the White Pass. The relatively small group who crossed in 1897 were so unprepared for life in the Yukon that the North West Mounted Police took control of the passes with machine guns in February 1898 and required every individual to carry at least 2,000 pounds of supplies. The average man could carry only a 50-pound pack, so this meant climbing the steep and icy pass 40 times. Many women made the journey, and those who did, often took off their long, cumbersome dresses and climbed in their bloomers, a kind of underwear similar to pants. Some women operated successful businesses during the rush, and historians consider the Klondike Stampede a breakthrough for women that led to new freedom in the 20th century.

George Carmack, Skookum Jim, and Charlie cleared $150,000 in spring 1898, just before the big wave of stampeders arrived. They leased out their claims and took a trip to Seattle and San Francisco that was supposed to be a celebration but only emphasized the differences between George and his Indian friends. In 1900, Carmack left Kate and married a white woman he had met at Dawson. Around the same time, he signed over his claims to Jim and broke off his relationship with Jim and Charlie.

*This story is based on Jim's account as told by William Ogilvie in* Early Days on the Yukon *and various source materials gathered in* Skookum Jim, *by Rab Wilkie and* The Skookum Jim Friendship Centre. *I have also used information from two excellent historical works,* Gold at Fortymile Creek, *by Michael Gates, and* The Klondike Fever, *by Pierre Berton.*

# BIBLIOGRAPHY

*The following bibliography is organized according to the ten stories. Each story bibliography is divided into two sections: the books actually used in developing and writing the story and the sources for all direct quotes in the story.*

*The quotes are identified by the speaker or writer, if this is clear in the text, followed by a colon (Speaker:) then a few words of the quote and the source in which it appears. For some quotes the name of the individual who provided the information appears in parentheses at the end of the listing, if this is not clear in the text.*

● ● ●

## BIG RIVER (pages 8–17)

Clarke, Charles G. *The Men of the Lewis and Clark Expedition.* Arthur H. Clark Co., Glendale, Calif.: 1970.

Moulton, Gary, ed. *The Journals of the Lewis and Clark Expedition.* 13 vols. University of Nebraska Press, Lincoln: 1983–2001.

Wheeler, Olin D. *The Trail of Lewis and Clark, 1804–1904.* 2 vols. G.P. Putnam's Sons, New York, N.Y.: 1926.

QUOTES: All quotes except Joseph Whitehouse's are from William Clark's journals for Oct. 23–Nov. 3, 1805, as published in Moulton, vol. 5. Whitehouse quotes are from Moulton, vol. 11. Clark: "was the whorls…" and "I deturmined…" pp. 331–33; "neeter made…" p. 328; "a verry bad place" p. 333; "extreamly gratified…" p. 338; "friendly Village" p. 351; "the water of this great river…" p. 363. Whitehouse: "The fairness…" p. 370; "made signs…" p.378.

## NO WATER (pages 18–27)

Brooks, George R., ed. *The Southwest Expedition of Jedediah S. Smith.* Arthur H. Clark Co., Glendale, Calif.: 1977. Reprint, University of Nebraska Press, Lincoln: 1989.

Morgan, Dale L. *Jedediah Smith and the Opening of the West.* Bobbs-Merrill Company, New York, N.Y.: 1953. Reprint, University of Nebraska Press, Lincoln: 1964.

Weber, David J. *The Californios versus Jedediah Smith, 1826–1827.* Arthur H. Clark Co., Spokane, Wash.: 1990.

QUOTES: All quotes are from Smith's journal as published in Brooks. "As it was useless…" pp. 51–2; "to my great Surprise…" p. 52; "The probability…" p. 53; "could hardly believe…" p. 57; "close at hand" and "indifferent… to him…" p. 58; "Colorado…" p. 66; "with great kindness" p. 72; "I expected to find…" pp. 77–8; "into the desert…" p. 79; "dry rocky sandy…" p. 88; "fine herds…" and "As those sure evidences…" pp. 93–4; "all the precaution…" p. 95; "how indians…" p. 98; "seemed to us…" and "interminable waste…" p. 96; "to be the first…" p. 37.

## INDEPENDENCE DAY (pages 28–37)

Drury, Clifford M. *Marcus and Narcissa Whitman and the Opening of Old Oregon.* 2 vols. Arthur H. Clark Co., Glendale, Calif.: 1973. Reprint, Pacific Northwest National Parks & Forests Assoc., Seattle, Wash.: 1986.

_____, ed. *Where Wagons Could Go.* Originally published as volume one of *First White Women Over the Rockies.* Arthur H. Clark Co., Glendale, Calif.: 1963. Reprint with new title and introduction by Julie Roy Jeffrey, University of Nebraska Press, Lincoln: 1997.

Gray, William Henry. *A History of Oregon, 1792–1849.* 1870. Reprint, Arno Press, New York, N.Y.: 1973.

Jeffrey, Julie Roy. *Converting the West: A Biography of Narcissa Whitman.* University of Oklahoma Press, Norman: 1991.

QUOTES: All quotes are from letters in Drury, *Where Wagons Could Go,* unless otherwise identified. Narcissa Whitman: "My health…" p. 57; "As soon…" p. 58; "It was truly…" pp. 58–9; "an unheard of journey…" p. 47; "If we had…" p. 68; "The Nez Perce…" p. 110; "steak…" Drury, *Marcus and Narcissa,* vol. 1, p. 198. Marcus Whitman: "They were greatly…" p. 68; "I see no reason…" p. 115. Henry Spalding: "Never send…" pp. 114–15. Thomas McKay: "There is something…" p. 116 (Spalding). William Gray: all quotes, Gray, pp. 118–23.

# BIBLIOGRAPHY

**I HAVE FOUND IT!** (pages 38–47)

Bancroft, Hubert Howe, *California inter Pocula*. Bancroft's Works, vol. 35. The History Co., Publishers, San Francisco, Calif.: 1888.

Gay, Theressa. *James W. Marshall*. Talisman Press, Georgetown, Calif.: 1967.

Gudde, Erwin G. *Bigler's Chronicle of the West*. University of California Press, Berkeley and Los Angeles: 1962.

Paul, Rodman W. *The California Gold Discovery*. Talisman Press, Georgetown, Calif.: 1966.

Smith, Azariah. *The Gold Discovery Journal of Azariah Smith*. Edited by David L. Bigler. University of Utah Press, Salt Lake City: 1990.

QUOTES: All quotes unless otherwise identified are from documents in Paul, *The California Gold Discovery*. James Marshall: "This is…" p. 170 (Brown); Marshall-Brown dialogue: pp. 168, 170 (Brown); "Tonight we will…" p. 168 (Brown); "Throw in a little…" p. 156 (Bigler); "about half past seven…" and Marshall-Scott dialogue: p. 118 (Marshall). Brown: "I wonder…" p. 164 (Bigler); "Gold!…" p. 172 (Brown). Bigler: "I must…" Gay, p. 150 (Brown); original diary entry, Paul, p. 62. Marshall-Sutter dialogue: Bancroft, pp. 70–2; Paul, pp. 125–9; and Gay, pp. 153–5 (Sutter). Sutter: "on very important…" Paul, p. 60.

**BLOOD ON THE TRAIL** (pages 48–59)

"Man Afraid of His Horses." Deposition, signed by O.F. Winship. Letters Received, January 1849 to December 1860. Department of the West, Record Group 98, United States Army Commands, Records of the War Department, National Archives, Washington, D.C.

*The Massacre of Lieutenant Grattan and his command by Indians*. Foreword by Paul L. Hedren. Introduction to plates by Carroll Friswold. Drawings by Black Horse. Arthur H. Clark Co., Glendale, Calif.: 1983.

Kappler, Charles J., ed. and comp. *Indian Treaties 1778–1883*. 1904. Reprint, Amereon House, Mattituck, N.Y.: 1972.

McCann, Lloyd E. "The Grattan Massacre." Nebraska History 37, no. 1 (March 1956). Reprint, Fort Laramie National Historic Site.

Nadeau, Remi. *Fort Laramie and the Sioux Indians*. Prentice-Hall, Englewood Cliffs, N.J.: 1967.

U.S. Congress. House. House of Representatives Reports, no. 63. 33rd Cong., 2nd sess., 1855. Doc. 788.

U.S. Congress. Senate. Report of the Secretary of War. 34th Cong., 1st sess., 1856. Ex. Doc. 91.

Watkins, Albert, ed. *Publications of the Nebraska State Historical Society*, vol. 20, pp. 259–68. Nebraska State Historical Society, Lincoln: 1922.

QUOTES: Man: "The young officer…" Man Afraid Deposition. Lucien: "You do not believe…" and "The Sioux…" McCann, pp. 11, 13 (Frank Salway). Grattan-Allen dialogue: U.S. Congress, Senate, p. 23 (Major Ed. Johnson). Grattan: "Men I don't believe…" ibid. Conquering Bear: "I must…"; Bordeaux-Grattan dialogue; Man: "My friend, come on…" all U.S. Congress, Senate, pp. 5–7 (James Bordeau[x]). Conquering Bear: "To day the Soldiers…" Man Afraid Deposition. "The right of the United States Government…" Kappler, p. 594. Benton: "sending our school-house officers…" Nadeau, p. 109. [Note: Some sources give the interpreter's name as Lucien Auguste, but the evidence suggests it was Auguste Lucien.]

**THEY'RE OFF!** (pages 60–71)

Bloss, Roy S. *Pony Express—The Great Gamble*. Howell-North, Berkeley, Calif.: 1959.

Chapman, Arthur. *The Pony Express*. G.P. Putnam's Sons, New York, N.Y.: 1932.

Godfrey, Anthony. *Historic Resource Study: Pony Express National Historic Trail*. United States Department of the Interior/National Park Service, Washington, D.C.: 1994.

Hauck, Louise Platt. "The Pony Express Celebration." *Missouri Historical Review* XLVII (July 1923), pp. 435–39.

*St. Joseph Free Democrat*, April 7, 1860.

*St. Joseph Gazette*, April 11, 1938. Interview with Billy Richardson.

*St. Joseph Weekly West*, April 7, 1860.

Settle, Raymond W. and Mary L. *Saddles & Spurs*. Stackpole Company, Harrisburg, Pa.: 1955. Reprint, University of Nebraska Press, Lincoln: 1972.

Smith, Waddell F., ed. *The Story of the Pony Express*. Pony Express History and Art Gallery, San Rafael, Calif.: 1960. Post Centennial Edition, 1964.

Sutro, Adolph, "A Trip to Washoe," in *Daily Alta Californian*, April 14, 1860.

Thompson, M. Jeff. Speech, April 3, 1860. Typescript.

QUOTES: "fine bay mare" *St. Joseph Weekly West*. "the little pony..." *St. Joseph Free Democrat*. M. Jeff Thompson: "I say..." Typescript. "a Mr. Richardson..." *St. Joseph Weekly West*. Billy Richardson: "just nosing..." *St. Joseph Gazette*. "a clean-limbed..." *San Francisco Bulletin*, April 3, 1860 (in Chapman, p. 115). "The storm..." Sutro.

## A RAILROAD TO THE MOON
(pages 72–83)

Bain, David Haward. *Empire Express*. Penguin Books, New York, N.Y.: 1999.

Best, Gerald M. *Iron Horses to Promontory*. Golden West Books, San Marino, Calif.: 1969.

Bowman, J.N. "Driving the Last Spike: At Promontory, 1869." *California Historical Society Quarterly* 36 (1957), pp. 97–106, 263-74. San Francisco, Calif.

Currier, John Charles. Personal diary. Golden Spike National Historic Site (GSNHS) Web site (http://www.nps.gov/gosp).

Griswold, Wesley S. *A Work of Giants*. McGraw-Hill Book Co., New York, N.Y.: 1962.

Kraus, George. *High Road to Promontory*. American West Publishing Co., Palo Alto, Calif.: 1969.

*New York Times*, May 9–12, 1869.

*Salt Lake Daily Telegraph*, May 11, 1869. GSNHS Web site.

Stillman, J.D.B. "The Last Tie." *Overland Monthly* 3 (July 1869). GSNHS Web site

QUOTES: "to build..." Bain, p. 18. "By nine o'clock..." *Sacramento Union*, May 10, 1869 (in Bain, p. 654). "with a black velvet..." Stillman. "Almost ready..." Bain, p. 665. "As we uncovered..." Stillman. "We have got done..." Bain, p. 665. "The Last Spike..." Best, p. 58. Dodge: "The great Benton..." and Durant: "There is henceforth..." *New York Times*, May 12, 1869. "carefully polished" Bowman, p. 105. "We all yelled..." Bain, p. 756, n. 31. Currier: "Champagne flowed..." Currier, diary, May 10, 1869.

## WE SHOOT, WE RIDE FAST, WE SHOOT AGAIN (pp. 84–97)

Camp, Walter. *Custer in '76*. Edited by Kenneth Hammer. Brigham Young University, Provo, Utah: 1976. New edition. University of Oklahoma Press, Norman: 1990.

Fox, Richard Allan, Jr. *Archaeology, History, and Custer's Last Battle*. University of Oklahoma Press, Norman: 1993.

Gardner, Mark L. *Little Bighorn Battlefield National Monument*. Southwest Parks and Monuments Assoc., 1996.

Graham, W.A., ed. and comp. *The Custer Myth*. Stackpole Co., Harrisburg, Pa.: 1953. Reprint, University of Nebraska Press, Lincoln: 1986.

Gray, John S. *Centennial Campaign*. Old Army Press, Fort Collins, Colo.: 1976.

_____. *Custer's Last Campaign*. University of Nebraska Press, Lincoln: 1991.

Hutton, Paul Andrew, ed. *The Custer Reader*. University of Nebraska Press, Lincoln: 1992.

Sklenar, Larry. *To Hell with Honor*. University of Oklahoma Press, Norman: 2000.

Utley, Robert M. *Little Bighorn Battlefield*. National Park Service, Washington, D.C.: 1994.

QUOTES: "worms crawling..." and Custer-Boyer dialogue: Camp, pp. 60–61, n. 2–3 (Lt. Charles Varnum). "cloud-like objects" Camp, p. 84 (Lt. Charles DeRudio). Custer order: "charge the village..." Sklenar, p. 147

(Reno). Kate Bighead: "We found our…west of the camp" Hutton, p. 366; "pushed the point" ibid., p. 376. "at will" Utley, p. 56 (Fred Gerard). Reno: "The very earth…" Gardner, p. 10. "Benteen. Come on…" ibid., p. 11 (Lt. William Cooke). Daniel Kanipe: "The boys began…" and Custer: "Hold your horses…" Gray, *Custer's Last*, p. 334. "The shooting at first…" Gardner, p. 12 (Wooden Leg). Two Moons: "Then the shooting…" Graham, p. 103. "We saw…" Gray, *Custer's Last*, p. 321 (Lt. Winfield Edgerly). Benteen: "They pounded…" Utley, p. 70.

**THROW UP YOUR HANDS!**
(pages 98–109)
Marks, Paula Mitchell. *And Die in the West.* William Morrow and Co., New York, N.Y.: 1989.
Tefertiller, Casey. *Wyatt Earp.* John Wiley & Sons, New York, N.Y.: 1997.
*Tombstone Epitaph*, October 27, 1881.
*Tombstone Nugget*, October 27, 1881.
Turner, Alford E., ed. *The O.K. Corral Inquest.* Creative Publishing Co., College Station, Texas: 1981.
Waters, Frank. *The Earp Brothers of Tombstone.* Clarkson N. Potter, New York, N.Y.: 1960.
QUOTES: All quotes are from Turner, *The O.K. Corral Inquest*, unless otherwise indicated. Ike-Wyatt dialogue no. 1: p. 160 (Wyatt Earp). Virgil-Allie dialogue: Waters, p. 155 (Allie Earp). Ike Clanton: "As soon as…" Turner, p. 174 (E.F. Boyle). Doc Holliday: "If God will let me…" p. 62, n. 2 (Kate Elder). Ike-Wyatt dialogue no. 2: p. 204 (R.J. Campbell). "25 armed men…" p. 195 (Virgil Earp). "You need not be afraid…" p. 29 (R.F. Coleman). Morgan-Doc dialogue: p. 40 (Martha J. King). Virgil Earp: "Boys…that!" p. 193 (Virgil Earp.) "had the impression" p. 31 (R.F. Coleman). Doc-Frank dialogue: *Tombstone Nugget.* Doc: "I am shocked…" Turner, p. 30 (R.F. Coleman). "stood up and fired…" *Tombtone Epitaph* (R.F. Coleman). Billy Clanton: "Good-bye boys…" *Tombstone Nugget* "The feeling…" *Tombtone Epitaph*

(John Clum). Wyatt Earp: "men of…" Tefertiller, p. 32. Judge Spicer: "a necessary act…" Turner, p. 225.

**GOLD! GOLD! GOLD!** (pp. 110–121)
Adney, Tappan. *The Klondike Stampede.* Harper & Brothers Publishers, New York, N.Y.: 1900. Reprint, with new introduction by Ken Coates. UBC Press, Vancouver, Can.: 1994.
Berton, Pierre. *The Klondike Fever.* Alfred A. Knopf, New York, N.Y.: 1958. Revised edition, *Klondike*, Penguin Books Canada, Toronto: 1972.
Cruikshank, Julie. *Life Lived Like a Story.* University of Nebraska Press, Lincoln: 1990.
Gates, Michael. *Gold at Fortymile Creek.* UBC Press, Vancouver, British Columbia, Can.: 1994.
Johnson, James Albert. *Carmack of the Klondike.* Epicenter Press, Seattle, Wash. and Horsdal & Schubart, British Columbia, Can.: 1990. New edition. *George Carmack*, Epicenter Press, Kenmore, Wash.: 2001.
Ogilvie, William. *Early Days on the Yukon.* John Lane Co., New York, N.Y.: 1913. Reprint, Arno Press, New York, N.Y.: 1974.
Wilkie, Rab, and The Skookum Jim Friendship Centre. *Skookum Jim.* Heritage Branch, Department of Tourism, Government of the Yukon, Whitehorse, Yukon, Can.: 1992.
QUOTES: Berton references are from *The Klondike Fever*. Skookum Jim's dream dialogue: Cruikshank, pp. 57–62 (Angela Sidney). Carmack: "a very vivid…" and "They were two beautiful fish…" Wilkie, p. 164; " damned Siwashes" Berton, p. 43. "his childish unreasoning prejudice…" Gates, p. 137; "reached down… hula-hula" Wilkie, pp. 85–7; "a trip…" ibid., p. 87; "human pin cushions" Gates, p. 138; "I felt…" Berton, p. 49. "moose pasture" Berton, p. 53. "GOLD! GOLD!…" *The Seattle Post-Intelligencer*, July 19, 1897 (in Berton, p. 106).

# CREDITS

Cover, clockwise from upper left: Richard Schlecht; H. Tom Hall; John F. Clymer, Courtesy Doris Clymer and the Clymer Museum of Art; National Anthropological Archives, Smithsonian Institution, Neg. #3678; Courtesy Library of Congress, Neg. LC-USZ62-44079; Alaska State Library, P. E. Larss Collection, Neg. #PCA 41-35; Bruce R. Greene, Courtesy Talei Publishers, Inc.; Cody Patrick Lyons Collection; Charles Hargens, Pony Express Museum, St. Joseph, Missouri; Courtesy of the California History Room, California State Library, Sacramento, California, Neg. #24,623; 4, Courtesy Scotts Bluff National Monument; 8, Richard Schlecht; 11 (both), Charles Willson Peale, Independence National Historic Park, photograph by James E. Russell; 12, Paul Kane, with permission of the Royal Ontario Museum © ROM; 15, Clark's Journal, c. Jan. 30, 1806, Voorhis #2, Clark Family Collection, William Clark papers, Missouri Historical Society Archives, photograph by Dick Durrance; 18, H. Tom Hall; 20, Reprinted from Anthony Finley's *New American Atlas*, 1826; 22, Denver Public Library, Western History Collection, #M-1159; 24, Ferdinand Deppe, Santa Barbara Mission Archive-Library; 28, John F. Clymer, Courtesy Doris Clymer and the Clymer Museum of Art; 30 (both), Courtesy of Whitman Mission National Historic Site; 32, Alfred Jacob Miller, The Walters Art Museum, Baltimore; 38, Charles Christian Nahl, Courtesy of the California History Room, California State Library, Sacramento, California, Neg. #24,623; 41, Arthur Nahl, Courtesy of the Bancroft Library, University of California, Berkeley; 43, Courtesy of the California History Room, California State Library, Sacramento, California, Neg. #908; 45, 46 (#1963.002:0052-B), Courtesy of the Bancroft Library, University of California, Berkeley; 48, Reprinted by permission of the Publishers, The Arthur H. Clark Company, from *The Massacre of Lieutenant Grattan*, edited by Paul Hedren, Glendale, Calif. 1983; 53, National Anthropological Archives, Smithsonian Institution, Neg. #3678; 54, Fort Laramie National Historic Site; 57, Reprinted by permission of the Publishers, The Arthur H. Clark Company, from *The Massacre of Lieutenant Grattan*, edited by Paul Hedren, Glendale, Calif. 1983; 60, Charles Hargens, Pony Express Museum, St. Joseph, Missouri; 64, 65, St. Joseph Museum, St. Joseph, Missouri; 66, *The Story of the Pony Express*, by Waddell F. Smith; 68, *Echoes from the Rocky Mountains*, by John W. Clampitt; 69, St. Joseph Museum, St. Joseph, Missouri; 70, Courtesy Library of Congress, Neg. LC USZ62-127508; 72, The Andrew J. Russell Collection, the Oakland Museum of California; 75, Courtesy of the California History Room, California State Library, Sacramento, California, Neg. #8527; 76, Courtesy of the Adirondack Museum; 79, The Granger Collection, New York; 81, Golden Spike National Historic Site; 82, Courtesy Library of Congress, Neg. LC-USZ62-44079; 84, Red Horse, National Anthropological Archives, Smithsonian Institution, INV 08569200, photograph by Mark Thiessen; 86, Cody Patrick Lyons Collection; 87, U.S. Army Military History Institute; 90, White Bird, West Point Museum Collection, U.S. Military Academy, photograph by Steven P. Zerby; 93, Reproduced from *A Pictographic History of the Oglala Sioux*, by Amos Bad Heart Bull, text by Helen H. Blish, published by the University of Nebraska Press; 94, Courtesy Little Bighorn Battlefield National Monument, National Park Service, Neg. #15394; 98, Courtesy of the Arizona Historical Society / Tucson, #17483; 100, Western History Collections, University of Oklahoma Library; 101, Collection of the New-York Historical Society, Neg. # 40746 (detail); 103 (all), Western History Collections, University of Oklahoma Library; 105, 107, Bruce R. Greene, Courtesy Talei Publishers, Inc.; 110, Photograph by E.A. Hegg, Alaska State Library, P.E. Larss Collection, Neg. #PCA 41147; 112, (left), Skookum Jim Oral History Project, Yukon Archives; 112, (right), 117, J. Johnson Collection, Yukon Archives; 119, Photograph by E.A. Hegg, Alaska State Library, James Wickersham Collection, Neg. #PCA 277-1-80; 120, Alaska State Library, P.E. Larss Collection, Neg. #PCA 41-35.

BACK JACKET QUOTES (for complete reference, see author entries listed in the Bibliography) Meriwether Lewis: *The Journals of the Lewis and Clark Expedition*, Moulton, vol. 4, p. 9; Narcissa Whitman: *Where Wagons Could Go*, Drury, p. 47; Sitting Bull: from *Sitting Bull, Champion of the Sioux*, by Stanley Vestal, rev. ed., University of Oklahoma Press, Norman: 1957, pp. 191–2.

# INDEX

Book design by Greaney Design
Text is set in Caslon; title type is set in Brothers and Saracen.
Tombstone map adapted with permission from Glenn G. Boyer. All other maps unless otherwise credited were created under the direction of Carl Mehler, Director of Maps; map research and production by Martin S. Walz.

Library of Congress Cataloging-in-Publication Data
Walker, Paul Robert.
 True tales of the Wild West / by Paul Robert Walker.
   p. cm.
Includes bibliographical references and index.
 ISBN 0-7922-8218-3
 1. West (U.S.)--History--Anecdotes--Juvenile literature. 2. West (U.S.)--Biography--Anecdotes--Juvenile literature. 3. Frontier and pioneer life--West (U.S.)--Anecdotes--Juvenile literature. [1. West (U.S.)--History. 2. Frontier and pioneer life--West (U.S.)] I. Title.
 F591 .W257 2002
 978'.02'0922--dc21

                                    2001008240

Printed in the United States of America

One of the world's largest nonprofit scientific and educational organizations, the National Geographic Society was founded in 1888 "for the increase and diffusion of geographic knowledge." Fulfilling this mission, the Society educates and inspires millions every day through its magazines, books, television programs, videos, maps and atlases, research grants, the National Geographic Bee, teacher workshops, and innovative classroom materials. The Society is supported through membership dues, charitable gifts, and income from the sale of its educational products. This support is vital to National Geographic's mission to increase global understanding and promote conservation of our planet through exploration, research, and education.

For more information, please call 1-800-NGS LINE (647-5463) or write to the following address:

**NATIONAL GEOGRAPHIC SOCIETY**
1145 17th Street N.W.
Washington, D.C. 20036-4688 U.S.A.

Visit the Society's Web site: www.nationalgeographic.com